THE MANY WAYS OF SEEING

An Introduction to the Pleasures of Art

THE MANY WAYS
OF SEEING

An Introduction to
the Pleasures of Art

Janet Gaylord Moore

THE WORLD PUBLISHING COMPANY
Cleveland and New York

PUBLISHED BY THE WORLD PUBLISHING COMPANY
2231 WEST 110TH STREET, CLEVELAND, OHIO 44102

PUBLISHED SIMULTANEOUSLY IN CANADA BY
NELSON, FOSTER & SCOTT LTD.

Library of Congress catalog card number: 67–23348

Acknowledgments

The writer would like to express a sense of indebtedness in the preparation of this book to many members of the curatorial staff at the Cleveland Museum of Art; to the Director, Sherman E. Lee; to James R. Johnson, Curator, Department of Art History and Education; and to Thomas Munro, the former Curator. Her thanks go also to Janet Mack, Margaret Marcus, Martin Linsey, Merald Wrolstad, to Richard Godfrey who made most of the black-and-white photographs, and to Ann Daniels and Dolores Filak for their help in preparing the manuscript.

Some of the ideas expressed grew out of a dozen teaching years in the spacious studios at Laurel School in Shaker Heights. Others go back to student days under the painter George Grosz.

Several chapters were written within view of a rather compelling slice of nature where,

> From the wide window towards the granite shore
> The white sails still fly seaward, seaward flying—
> Unbroken wings
>
> —T. S. Eliot

J. G. M.
Stonington, Maine
August, 1967

To all the students
who have been my teachers

Contents

Color Illustrations

Preface

We are proud of our high "rate of literacy"; I suspect we secretly sigh or, worse, snicker, when we read of this or that people with negligible or non-existent literacy. Despite current attempts to magnify the effects of "non-linear," non-literate methods of communication, one cannot be wrong in saying that the ability to spell C-A-T lies at the base of the little wisdom or understanding we now possess. The overwhelming educational effort of developed civilization, whether Occidental or Oriental, has been to inculcate literacy.

During modern times, something like the same effort has been made to develop scientific and mathematical "literacy" within developed civilizations. $E=mc^2$ is certainly as well known as *The Wasteland,* and would be as well known as *Macbeth,* had it been allowed equal elapsed time for existence.

I hope, then, that it comes as a shock to know that Westerners, and many Orientals, are visually illiterate. If asked to spell the visual equivalent of such a simple proposition as C-A-T and to describe what the combination signified, an overwhelming majority, perhaps over ninety percent, of those asked would not even know where to begin. Especially in the twentieth century, with the development of "Education" as a discipline for mass indoctrination in the knowledge of mankind, visual education—the base for any beginning knowledge of, or skill in, art—has had but a sub-minor role. If M. Dubois speaks to Mr. Jones and the sounds do not "make sense," Mr. Jones does not immediately assume that M. Dubois is either crazy or putting him on. In at least a majority of cases Mr. Jones will understand that the exotic M. Dubois is speaking a language different from his own, and further, that to understand one another, one must undertake to learn the language of the other. As to which language is "better," the question does not arise—it simply is a matter of learning in order to understand. But if Mr. Jones sees a painting by Mr. Kelly, or the design of a city by Mr.

Soleri, he has no hesitation in considering them both either crazy or capricious and, worse, unworthy of attention.

But the fact of the matter is that Mr. Jones is "illiterate" in visual language. Giotto, Rembrandt, Cézanne, *and* Rauschenberg are simply "speaking" a foreign language which our educational system makes little effort to include in the curriculum. There can be no change in our visual environment until this particular language becomes a part of our accepted culture rather than being relegated to "rest and recreation."

This is what Janet Moore's book is all about. It is an introduction to vision with reference to the visual arts—a primer if you will, but because it is just that, a must for most adults, who unfortunately have never even passed first grade in visual education. This book has been most effective with the young and was written for them, in the sense that they were youthful beginners in the visual arts. It is a sensitive, sympathetic, and well-ordered introduction for all "youthful beginners" from eight to eighty, provided their minds are young enough to think of beginning. I hope that *The Many Ways of Seeing* and other books of similar intention and of equal merit become as widely read and understood as possible. Maybe then an important part of our environment, what we see, can begin to be improved—and by that I mean made fit for human consumption.

Sherman E. Lee
DIRECTOR, THE CLEVELAND MUSEUM OF ART

Introduction

There are many ways of seeing: with scientific observation, with intellectual detachment, with emotional involvement. Indeed it is hardly possible to separate these three. There are also the highly individual and personal ways of thinking and feeling that the master artists present to us. At different times in your own life you will find yourself attuned to the wave lengths of different artists. But the language of art through which these artists speak to us is not an open book as many people imagine. It is a language that we never finish learning, and for which this book hopes to provide a few clues.

The purpose of this book is to suggest ways of sharpening visual awareness and of cultivating perception in the visual arts; it is also to suggest some of the ways in which we look back and forth from the world of nature to the world of art. Since it is important that looking should not be altogether passive, there are simple exercises provided for those who have stage fright in front of a blank sheet of paper, or who find their own doodling somewhat monotonous. Pencils, pastels, or crayons and paper, along with that excellent instrument the camera, can help us find out what we see, can reinforce our seeing.

Although this is a book for young people, it is not meant as a text for anyone planning to become a professional artist. The training necessary for a painter, sculptor, architect, or designer should begin in more systematic ways, move more slowly and with more depth and discipline.

Our eyes today are bombarded with thousands of images from advertising, moving pictures, and television. All this makes more difficult than ever the task of cultivating a selective and discriminating eye. The ways in which you look at the world of nature and the world of art can help you understand yourself and what kind of person you choose to become. Your own experiences of life can, in turn, broaden and deepen your understanding of this language of the arts.

12

I

Observation and Perception

What do you see when you look? Suppose you are standing at the window on a rainy evening. Your attention might be caught by raindrops sliding against the outside of the pane, forming and reforming in vertical and diagonal patterns. But if you begin looking through the glass, you might see the wet, dark streets beyond, the pools of color; crimson, yellow, and blue reflections of neon lights; cars and people moving in dark silhouette against the lighted shops. It is impossible to look with equal attention at the pane of glass and at the distance beyond. The eye selects, or is it the mind that chooses?

In the same way that the dark cars and trucks slide in and out of your field of vision, other aspects of the city at night may swim through your consciousness—some sense of rainy nights remembered in other cities, perhaps curiosity about the little group of people huddled in the lighted doorway. Another level of your mind, half hypnotized by the changing lights, may see flower shapes in the wet pavement, purple and crimson anemones with their dark centers. Looking, thinking, feeling, remembering —how are they related? Can we ever separate them?

Do two people looking out over the same landscape see the same scene? Do our eyes constantly compose and recompose what is before us, focus down on detail and then open up for a wider view? What of the mysterious thought that the artist Franz Marc suggests: how does the world look to the eye of an animal?

We know that the eye can be trained and disciplined to many kinds of seeing. The scientist observing the most intricate variations in a complex structure—either with his own eyes or with a powerful instrument—sees details and relationships that would escape the rest of us. The pilot and the sailor, from long experience, are able to observe every hint and sign of wind, weather, and water. There is the skillful tennis player whose quickness of eye is equaled by quickness of hand. There is the artist whose perception of certain relationships of form and color enables him, not to copy what is before him, but to construct a pictorial equivalent for a landscape or a figure. The artist sometimes sees these relations of color and form without paying too much attention to what they represent. He may be able to forget "chair" as something to sit in and see dark pattern against light wall so that the meaning "chair" is less important than color, angle, light-and-dark pattern. He sees, we may say, with an "innocent eye." "To see," the poet Paul Valéry said, "is to forget the name of the thing one sees."

Sometimes the familiar can be made more extraordinary or unfamiliar by a change of scale. A magnifying glass or microscope can change a shell, a handful of pebbles, or a beetle into a new and amazing world. The marvelous resources of modern photography with microscopes and telescopes and X rays astonish us with unsuspected patterns and shapes.

But you yourself can also change the scale simply by lying down in the long grass and getting an ant's-eye view of the jungle close around you. Perhaps you can remember as a child some secret lair where tall grasses and ferns fenced in a hidden and private world.

The airplane provides us with patterns of earth and water and forms of clouds that have never been seen until our century. There is much in the art of our time that seems to be related to this new look of earth and sea, rivers, forests, and cities seen from the air. We have become accustomed not only to the textures and patterns of earth from the air but also to the freewheeling angles of vision provided by aerial photography.

It is true that we can sometimes see extraordinary effects when traveling at six hundred miles an hour or even at sixty miles an hour, but it is just possible that people who had to walk or ride horseback in order to travel were more observant, more thoughtful, more imaginative than we are. A long walk alone in the city or the country, perhaps with a camera or a sketchbook, is still one of the best ways of finding out what you are seeing, thinking, feeling, remembering.

If you live in a city it is important to get out into the country, or into a park, into the woods, onto the water, anywhere where you are in direct contact with the world of nature. The infinite variety of the forms of nature is a counterbalance to our mass-produced culture. Without such a personal awareness of nature's forms, many of the delights and rewards of painting, sculpture, and architecture will be forever lost to you.

The painter John Marin was speaking about artists when he wrote this, but it really applies to us all:

> Seems to me the true artist must perforce go from time to time to the elemental big forms, Sky, Sea, Mountain, Plain—and those things pertaining thereto, to sort of re-true himself up, to recharge the battery. For these big forms have everything. But to express these you have to love these, to be a part of these in sympathy.[1]

John Marin   MAINE ISLANDS

2

What the Artists Have Taught Us To See

First we see the hills in the painting, then we see the painting in the hills.

—Li Li-Wêng, Chinese, seventeenth century

Whether we are aware of it or not, our ways of seeing are affected by artists whose names or work we may never have known. If you have no opportunity to see original works of art in museums and galleries, you probably look at reproductions in books, magazines, newspapers, or on television. This is what the French writer André Malraux calls the "Museum Without Walls," the *"Musée Imaginaire."* Very often without suspecting it, you are seeing at second or third hand ideas or images that the truly original artists have been the first to express, ideas that other artists or designers, illustrators or advertisers, have appropriated and have spread far and wide.

In the first half of our century, the Dutch painter Piet Mondrian worked out his own austere and spare language of forms and colors from which everything superfluous had been stripped away. The language in which he speaks to us is made of horizontals and verticals balanced with extraordinary precision in stripes and rectangles of red, yellow, blue, black, and white (see page 63). For nearly fifty years industrial designers and illustrators have been borrowing ideas from Mondrian for everything from kitchen linoleums to advertising layout and, more recently, for fashion. This secondary use of the style of an artist or a group of artists often obscures for us the inventor's true originality.

There are other ways that artists affect the world around them. It is

16

easy to imagine that all the women and girls in the Paris of Auguste Renoir's day must have had round faces, shining eyes, and small noses. Renoir's son tells us that the vision the artist created was indeed so enchanting that after a while the women and girls with their soft hair, bright eyes, and ruffled costumes did begin to look like the paintings. We might paraphrase the quotation at the beginning of this chapter: "First we see the women in the paintings, then we see the paintings in the women."

Pierre Auguste Renoir THE LUNCHEON OF THE BOATING PARTY

A few years ago, I was standing on a dock in Venice after looking at a big international exhibit that is called the *Biennale*. A priest and a group of young people were waiting for the water-bus to come along. In obvious exasperation, the priest looked down at the splattered, paint-stained, torn linoleum at his feet and said, "You could put six square feet of this on the wall and they would call it a painting." He was very nearly right. But with-

Pierre Soulages PAINTING

out the kinds of paintings at which the group had been looking so scornfully they might never have noticed what was under their feet—that extraordinary variety of spattered color and texture glistening in the gray light of a wet Venetian afternoon.

Once, on a night train, as I looked out every now and then at black girders and signal towers against shifting lights, I seemed to see the strong black forms, the thrust and weight of paintings by Pierre Soulages, the last exhibit I had seen before leaving New York. This does not mean at all that Soulages was thinking of railways at night when he made the paintings; his paintings are untitled. It would be nearer the truth to say that the broad black strokes have to do with force and thrust and structure and balance, but the impact of such a painting can set up resonances in the world around us, can bring variety and interest to an ordinary journey.

There is a story about a girl on a railway train in England in the 1840's. She sat opposite an extraordinary little man who kept putting his head out of the window and staring into the rain and smoke. Finally he said to her, "You must absolutely put your head out of the window and see what I see." So she did. Some weeks later at the exhibition of the Royal Academy in London, this same girl heard a group of pompous gentlemen exclaiming in great indignation over a painting by J. M. W. Turner. "Whoever saw anything like that?" said one of them. "I did," replied the girl. "A gentleman on a train made me peer out of the window at the rain and the steam. I looked at what he saw and it was exactly like that." They were talking about "Rain, Steam, and Speed," which is now considered one of the masterpieces of English painting (see page 35).

A thousand years ago in China there were landscape painters who looked at great vertical mountains with their cliffs and waterfalls, their dense foliage half hiding Buddhist temples and village roofs. They sometimes saw also the tiny figure of a lonely woodchopper or a wandering scholar on a remote mountain path. By means of brush and ink, through a subtle and complex language of symbols, those painters were able to express the vastness of nature, the harmony of man with rock and tree, clouds and stream, in such a compelling way that Chinese artists, and many Japanese painters as well, have looked at their work as a living source and inspiration. Down through the centuries, other artists have quite consciously practiced variations on these great "mountain and water pictures," as the Chinese call landscape paintings, of the Sung Dynasty.

That is why a seventeenth-century Chinese writer could say, "First we

18

(Opposite) *Ch'ien Hsuan* EARLY AUTUMN (detail)

see the hills in the painting, then we see the painting in the hills." The painter's vision of the landscape became the Chinese idea of landscape.

There were also painters in China and Japan who thought about bamboo in the wind, about fish swimming upstream, about birds or peonies or insects. They set down their observations so masterfully that later generations of painters and poets could look at these smaller forms of nature with new insight and appreciation.

In the nineteenth century, Japanese art was still a new discovery for European artists, and very stimulating. In 1880, Vincent van Gogh wrote to his brother Theo:

> If we study Japanese art we see a man who is undoubtedly wise, philosophic and intelligent, who spends his time doing what? In studying the distance between the earth and the moon? No. In studying Bismarck's policy? No. He studies a single blade of grass.
>
> But this blade of grass leads him to draw every plant and then the seasons, the wide aspects of the countryside, then animals, then the human figure. So he passes his life, and life is too short to do the whole. . . .
>
> And you cannot study Japanese art, it seems to me, without becoming much gayer and happier, and we must return to nature in spite of our education and our work in a world of convention.[1]

3

On Looking at Paintings

Is a painting a picture window through which we look? Is it an object in itself?

Let us look at a painting by Van Gogh and think about what he saw and felt in the world of nature and what he adapted for his own purposes from the world of art. Out of this fusion he made the paintings that are so much admired today, paintings that seemed impossibly wild and strange when they were new. About the picture reproduced on page 38, Van Gogh wrote:

> I have a wheat field, very yellow and very light, perhaps the lightest canvas I have done.
>
> The cypresses are always occupying my thoughts, I should like to make something of them like the canvases of the sunflowers, because it astonishes me that they have not been done as I see them. [Here the writer inserted a pen sketch of a cypress tree.]
>
> It is as beautiful in line and proportion as an Egyptian obelisk.
>
> And the green has a quality of such distinction.
>
> It is a splash of *black* in a sunny landscape, but it is one of the most interesting black notes, and the most difficult to hit off exactly that I can imagine.
>
> But then you must see them against the blue, *in* the blue rather. To paint nature here, as everywhere, you must be in it a long time. . . .[1]

In the brilliant air of Southern France, so dazzling to a painter from Northern Europe, Van Gogh became obsessed with the idea of sunlight. The intensity of his own feeling led him to a strongly rhythmical, emotional movement of the brush and to a high-keyed expressive use of color for the forms of tree and cloud and field. Anyone can sense this much, I think, whether or not he knows anything at all about painting in the nineteenth century. But it may be interesting to know that Van Gogh began as a painter of dark peasant interiors in Holland, where he grew up. Later, in Paris, he came in contact with the challenging new ideas about color and light of a group of painters known as the Impressionists. Van Gogh experimented briefly with some of the Impressionist methods. But, in Provence, in the bright sunlit landscape of Southern France, he found, in a few short years of driving energy, his own way of working, the personal style that could express his own innermost feelings.

At the same time, in another part of Provence lived a quite different artist, Paul Cézanne. You have to look longer and more thoughtfully at a Cézanne landscape than at one painted by Van Gogh. Cézanne set himself a still more difficult task: to express with small planes of color the crystalline structure of the forms of rocks, trees, slopes, mountain, or sky. (His approach was the same whether painting landscape, still life, or figures.) He seems to have dissolved the landscape into a thousand fragments and yet has united the forms into a harmonious whole.

On the flat white canvas, Cézanne was able to create a sense of geometric forms or volumes in deep space by sensitively juxtaposing small patches of color. At the same time he was able to preserve the flat vertical quality of the surface of the canvas. This creates a tension, a pull between the deep space and the vertical surface so that a constant shift is going on before our eyes which makes the painting always seem alive. What I have tried to suggest is hard enough to grasp, and yet it is only the beginning of an understanding of Cézanne's art. But the point is this: a fine painting somehow always has a life of its own. We never see it twice in quite the same way. This is the secret of its compelling quality, the secret of a painting that lives no matter what its period or date.

Our discussion of painting has begun with Van Gogh and Cézanne because much of what has happened to painting since their time is easier to understand if we think of Van Gogh's expressive and emotional style and of Cézanne's search for order and harmony.

In some sense, then, painting, especially a landscape, may be a picture window through which we look. But if that is all it is, the reproduction of a particular view in nature, it will soon lose interest for us, it will have no power to renew itself before our eyes. The underlying order or organization, the echoes and repetitions of forms and colors, the rhythmical interweaving of lines, all these are elements an artist uses to command our attention and to arouse our feelings.

A painting may announce itself across a wide gallery even before we are close enough to make out the actual subject matter. In one of the galleries of the Prado Museum in Madrid, that wonderful collection of the kings of Spain, I was startled to see among the old masters a painting that appeared to be entirely abstract. From a distance I felt the rich, sonorous reds, the deep blues, the shadowy forms in a strange and somber harmony. When I came closer I saw that this was indeed an old master painting, Titian's "Entombment" (see page 36). Before it was possible to discern the subject, the atmosphere of the painting had sent out deep chords like the opening notes of a great symphony.

The small color reproduction of the Titian "Entombment" can, of course, give you only a partial impression of the painting itself. In the first place there is the question of size. The original painting is nearly seven feet wide. The mysterious movement of color in and out of shadow, the sense of the material itself, oil color on canvas with the melting edges of each tone, the appearance of depth in the layers of color right down to the canvas beneath, the movement of the brush or touch of the artist's hand, so different in the Titian, the Van Gogh, and the Cézanne—these are all lost to some extent in a reproduction, however fine it may be. And it is exactly through these qualities that the meaning and mood of this painting, its drama and pathos, are best conveyed.

You can understand, then, why it is important to see the original works of art whenever you can. The surface of a plaster cast, for instance, is a dead surface compared to the living marble, carved and polished by the Greek sculptor himself, even though the stone may have been damaged in the course of centuries.

But there is also a great advantage to the reproduction as a means of study, since we can make investigations and comparisons that are impossible in any other way. Through the study of reproductions, we may be able to build up experience which will enable us to look longer and with more awareness when we have a chance to see the original works of art.

4

How an Artist Holds Our Attention: Line, Color, and Form

Let us go back to a sentence in Chapter 3: "The underlying order or organization, the echoes and repetitions of forms and colors, the rhythmical interweaving of lines, all these are elements an artist uses to command our attention and to arouse our feelings." Reduced to their simplest terms, these elements may be described as line, color, and form.

LINE

If you make a dot and then place a series of dots right next to it in close succession, you will have a line. We can say that a line is a projected dot. We can also say that a dot is the end view of a line that moves directly away from us. Hold a pencil so that you can see its full length. The pencil represents a line. Now turn it so that you can see only the sharpened tip. By closing one eye as you look at it, you can see the pencil as a dot. Turn it full length again and you have a line.

Some lines seem to lie on the surface of the paper. Others appear to dive down into space, to surface again, to express movement and direction. It can be said that a line has derivation and destination, it is coming from somewhere and it is going somewhere. In his teaching at the Bauhaus School in Germany, the painter Paul Klee used to say to his students, "Take a walk with a line." He probably meant, start somewhere on your page and move with a lively curiosity over the whole surface in and out as one might ramble about on a country walk.

Some lines, especially pen lines, show the nervous energy of a hand moving rapidly. Lines made by a soft Chinese brush weighted with ink seem to express a crescendo and a diminuendo as the brush is guided

POINT

LINE

PLANE

23

through large slow curves or steered swiftly about. Other lines, drawn with a ruling pen or a hard pencil, are straight, sure, and accurate.

If you draw a line and imagine one line next to another tightly packed side by side, you would have what we call a plane, a plane surface, or flat area. A plane may be tilted or it may be irregular in shape, but the surface, the direction of the surface, does not vary.

If you remove the paper from a crayon—or better, use a lithographic crayon—on its side, and draw it sideways across a sheet of paper, you will have a more or less even tone representing a plane.

With these resources—a point, a line, a plane—the draftsman and the printmaker can produce work of great variety and richness.

Jean Honoré Fragonard
SCENE IN A PARK (detail at left)

As children, our first contact with the materials of an artist is usually with a crayon or a pencil scribbled round and round in a gleeful tangle. A little later we make outlines that represent head, body, arms, legs, or house. But there are many adults who never get beyond the idea of line as a bounding contour or outline. The contour line can be used with great power or with the most delicate subtlety, but it is only one of many ways in which lines may represent thoughts, ideas, and feelings.

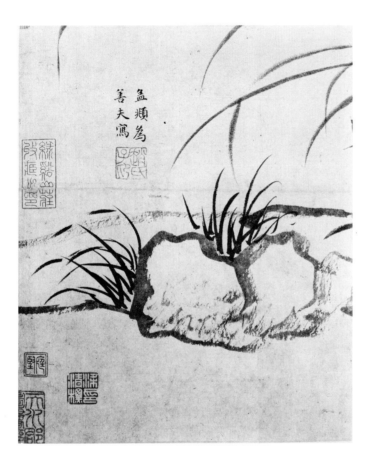

Chao Mêng-fu BAMBOOS, ROCKS, AND LONELY ORCHIDS (detail)

COLOR

How would you describe color to a person who has never been able to see? What would you say for instance about red? What comes to your mind when you hear the word? Is it the red of the blood in our veins, the red of roses, of fire engines, of sunsets, of a traffic light? We can hardly use the

25

word blue without being vaguely aware of sky and air. But there is also the familiar idea of "feeling blue." The paintings of Picasso's "blue period" are all in a melancholy mood. Yellow is the color we associate with sunlight, with radiance, with gold. It is the imperial color in China where the great palaces in Peking are roofed in bright yellow tile as if covered with ears of golden corn, row upon row.

We speak of red, yellow, and blue as the three primary colors; that is, you cannot make red, yellow, and blue out of any other colors. Anyone who has experimented with a box of colors knows that red and yellow make orange, that blue and yellow make green, and that red and blue make violet. Orange, green, and violet are known therefore as secondary colors.

Sometime when the sun is shining and rain is still falling, look hard—or should one say look softly?—at a rainbow. See if you can decide at what point red turns to orange, yellow to green, blue to violet. The sun shining through the raindrops breaks up light into the colors of the spectrum. The colors of the rainbow then are pure light. But artists must work with pigments, ground-up colors, which cannot be mixed with the brilliance and purity of light itself. All the colors of the spectrum mixed together make white light. With pigments, however, when we combine the complementary colors, red and green, blue and orange, yellow and violet, we get varying shades of gray instead of pure white. (These grays, made without any addition of black, are most useful to painters.)

Most color charts place red, yellow, and blue equidistant on a circle or color wheel. When colors are arranged in this way, one can easily see the pairing of opposites or complementary colors at any point on the color wheel. Skillful painters know how to enhance a color by placing its

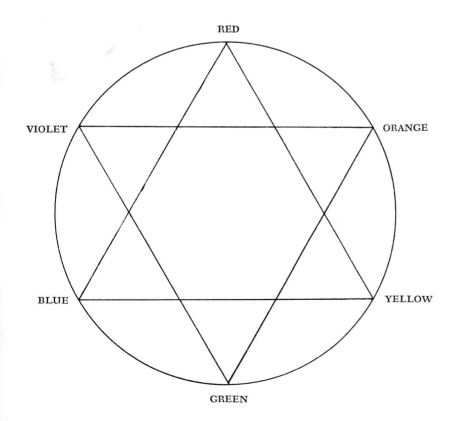

(Opposite) *Albert Pinkham Ryder* THE
RACE TRACK OR DEATH ON A PALE HORSE

complementary color close by. It is these oppositions that produce the most vibrant color effects. Van Gogh said, "I can hardly paint a yellow-green without painting a blue-violet." You can experiment with complementary colors for yourself by staring at a bright red square for a full minute or two and then closing your eyes. The afterimage on the inside of your eyelids will appear as a green square, the opposite or complementary color of the red.

Colors within the red-yellow-orange group are commonly called warm colors. The blue-green-violet group are designated as cool colors. This broad distinction is fairly obvious, but there are also most subtle distinctions between, say, a cool silvery gray and a warm pearly gray. It is generally held that cool colors tend to recede into the distance, that the reds and oranges appear to advance. Thus, colors may appear to advance or recede within what is called pictorial space. A knowledgeable painter commands this movement of color within pictorial space in somewhat the same way that an orchestra conductor controls the sounds and volume of the instruments.

When we want to speak of the relative lightness or darkness of a color in the scale from white to black we speak of *values*. Drawings and prints and many paintings depend for their effect not so much on color as on the relative values, the relation of tones from light to dark and the placement of these tones in the design or structure of the composition. The Albert P. Ryder painting reproduced below depends for its impact on the placement and proportion of light and dark tones.

Physicists and physiologists can tell us a great deal about the scientific aspects of color and how our eyes distinguish color. But still there is something deep in our feelings that responds emotionally to qualities of color, something elusive that even the psychologists can never quite explain. The great masters of color, from the mosaic artists of early Christian days to the designers of medieval stained glass, painters from Fra Angelico and Titian in the Renaissance to Monet and Matisse in modern times have known by intuition and investigation how to evoke these seemingly magical properties of color.

Some people who are disturbed or baffled by modern painting are perhaps unwilling to open their minds to the experience of color—to respond to color as naturally as they respond to certain kinds of music.

FORM

In any large dictionary you will find a number of meanings given for the word "form." Two of these meanings concern us in understanding works of art. The first is form as "shape." We may say that in each of the small rectangles of the photograph below there is a dark shape against a light background. We sometimes speak of this as figure and ground. The apparent forms or shapes are actually broken windowpanes, each one an interesting study in figure and ground. We speak also of three-dimensional forms. In the "Torso" by Constantin Brancusi we may say that the forms of the human body have been reduced to their simplest terms.

Constantin Brancusi TORSO   *Amedeo Modigliani* PORTRAIT OF A GIRL

The second or broader meaning of form has to do with the underlying order or organization of a composition, the structure or unifying rhythm that gives a work of art its special and unique character.

In reading about the visual arts—drawing, painting, sculpture, and architecture—you will sometimes find the phrase "formal relationships." In painting, the formal relationships—that is, the placement of shapes, the echoes of color, the rhythmic movement—are traditionally expressed on a flat surface, the vertical surface of a painting, whether that surface is canvas, a wood panel, or a wall.

In sculpture and architecture the forms actually exist in three-dimensional space as solids and voids or, we could say, as mass, planes, exterior and interior space, which may be unified in various ways: by the relations of masses (proportion), by rhythmic design, by the character of the surface, smooth or textured. The effect of light is of great importance in revealing to us the forms of sculpture and architecture.

29

(Opposite) BROKEN WINDOW PANES   *Photograph by Joseph McCullough*

When we discuss the broader meaning of form, that which contributes to the organization or unity of the whole, we find ourselves using a number of terms, among them:

Pattern, a regular repetition of lines, shapes, or colors.

Texture, which always suggests the sense of touch, that which is hard or soft, rough or smooth, bristling or silky. Textures may be actually touchable or tangible when carved in stone or cast in metal. They may be represented in various ways in drawings or paintings.

Composition, which comes from the Latin "putting together," the composing of all the various elements into a unified whole.

There are certain forms that are characteristic of an individual artist, such as the elongated ovals of the painter Amedeo Modigliani. Other forms are characteristic of whole periods and of individual artists within that period. We think of the tall pointed forms of the Gothic style of the fourteenth century in Europe or the swinging, dynamic curves of the baroque style of the seventeenth century. The gradual or sudden shifts in this "life of forms" is of great interest to art historians.

Peter Paul Rubens RUBENS WITH HIS
FIRST WIFE, ISABELLA BRANT

German, fifteenth century A BRIDAL PAIR

The style of an individual artist is the sum total of the characteristic forms that he uses to express his own ideas and feelings. The style of a period or country is made up of the characteristic forms used by the artists of the same general time and region. Often the minor artists are more typical of the style of their time and place than the great masters, whose mature work goes beyond the merely typical.

Let us think now about some of the ways in which certain paintings are composed or given form. Look at the two paintings on page 33 by French artists of the first half of the nineteenth century, Jean Auguste Dominique Ingres and Eugène Delacroix. If you will sketch a rectangle that corresponds in proportion to the height and width of the Ingres "Reclining Odalisque" and then try to express the general feeling of the linear rhythms in this painting, you cannot help arriving at a crescent shape played against vertical and horizontal lines.

You have tried a freehand diagram. Now lay a piece of tracing paper over the Ingres painting, turn the book upside down, and sketch the frame or borders of the picture. Then try to search out in more detail the main directions through which the eye is led within the painting. It is very important not to let yourself begin to trace around the light shape of the seated figure against the dark ground. That is too easy and altogether misses the point of this exercise. Look for the large curves, the horizontal and vertical lines that carry across from one edge of the painting to the other. Using a soft pencil, try to draw these movement with your whole arm and wrist, not just with the fingers as in writing. Turn your paper right side up

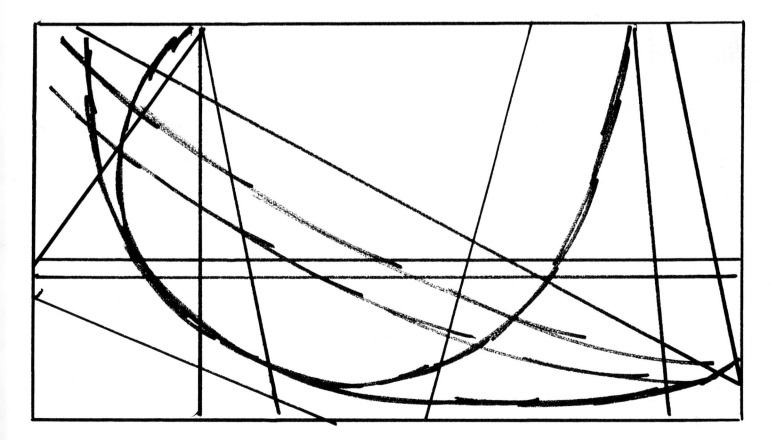

and compare the diagram with the painting. Does it seem to indicate, however crudely, the main directions through which the eye moves? Remember you are not copying or tracing the *picture,* you are searching for its structure, order, and rhythm. There are many ways of seeing a single painting like this elegant, elongated nude by a master of French classicist painting. At this point try to concentrate on the linear movement.

Then look at the "St. George and the Dragon" by Delacroix. (It may interest you to know that these two artists, although contemporaries, and both working in France, represented two opposing points of view and disliked each other intensely.) Again, sketch a rectangle that represents the proportions of height to width of the painting. Turn the book upside down and try to sketch the main movement and direction of the forms. The reason you turn "St. George" upside down is so your eye will not become

Fan K'uan TRAVELING AMONG STREAMS AND MOUNTAINS

J. M. W. Turner RAIN, STEAM, AND SPEED

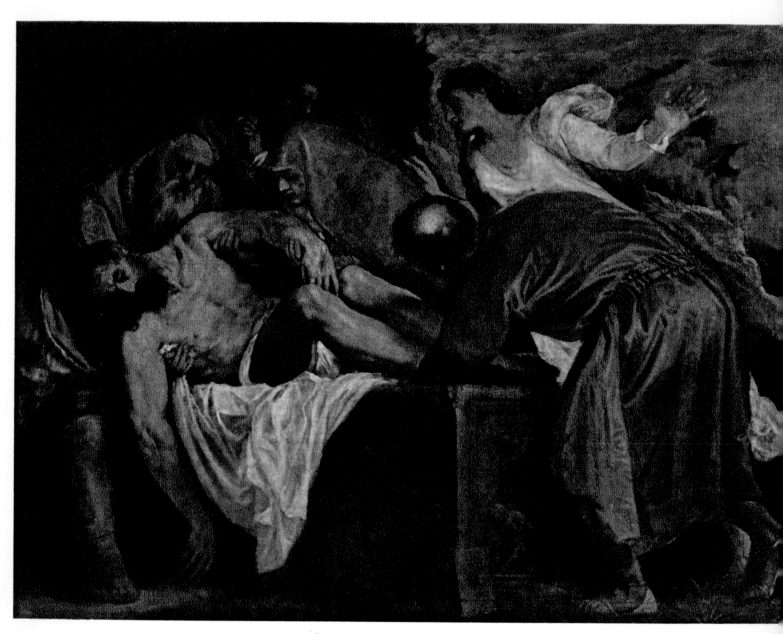

Titian THE ENTOMBMENT

Mark Rothko   BROWN AND BLACK ON PLUM

Vincent van Gogh   WHEAT FIELD WITH CYPRESSES

Paul Cézanne   THE PIGEON TOWER AT MONTBRIAND

Edouard Manet THE FIFER

Claude Monet ANTIBES

Rembrandt van Rijn   SELF-PORTRAIT

too involved with subject matter, but will concentrate on the flowing and spiraling movements that give the painting its special character or style. You will find the contours less sharply defined than in the Ingres.

After that preliminary diagram, lay tracing paper over the picture, and indicate the boundaries of the painting. Again turn the book upside down and let your hand move freely over the light and dark areas as you search for whatever gives continuity to the forms within this composition. (With a painting as dark as this, you will have to look under the tracing paper from time to time.) It is interesting to take a ruler and look for anchorage points or accents that hold your eye to a definite vertical, horizontal, or diagonal line. It takes practice to see the skeleton or structure underneath the more obvious subject matter of the painting. We should never suppose we have discovered an exact plan on which a painting is laid out. The master painters are too subtle, too full of surprises for us to analyze their method so easily. But the search can sharpen your own seeing.

Go back to your studies of linear movement in the two paintings. Lay the diagrams over the reproduction and try to add the main dark areas by indicating their forms with an even tone. You are investigating still another element in the formal design, the pattern of light and dark shapes. You can also try to see the movement of the eye in depth. The Ingres is clearly flatter than the Delacroix.

You should be able to sense that color is used in different ways by these two artists. In the Ingres "Odalisque" the colors of each area are held within clear boundaries. There are no exaggerations, no daring liberties taken with the color. The subordination of color to the drawing and to the carefully planned composition are characteristic of the neoclassical style to which this painting belongs. The term neoclassical means "new classical," a style that was thought to be a revival of Greek and Roman discipline after the exuberant frivolities of eighteenth-century court art. The only exaggerations are in the drawing of the figure, the long drawn-out curve of the body, the length of the spinal column. Ingres felt that drawing was more important than color, which he said was a mere icing on the cake.

In the painting by Delacroix, on the other hand, color moves, leaps, sparkles, subsides, dissolves, and builds up again. The clear outlines of the drawing, if they ever existed, are lost in the transitions and interactions of color. The composition is restless, dynamic, full of drama and energy. This is characteristic of the "romantic" style in painting.

The art historian Heinrich Wölfflin made current the pair of words

41

"linear" and "painterly," which are useful in defining two ways of working. It is not hard to see that we could apply the word "linear" to the style of Ingres, the word "painterly" to the style of Delacroix.

It has been said that three elements enter into the experience of looking at works of art. First there is the style of an individual artist, second, the style of his time, and third, the perception and experience that the viewer brings to the activity of seeing. In a sense the viewer re-creates a work of art for himself in the same way that a musician interprets a musical score.

We have touched on the style of an individual artist in speaking of Titian, of Van Gogh and Cézanne, of Ingres and Delacroix. Although an artist's way of working may change and evolve as he grows older, there is usually a certain personal, recognizable quality that distinguishes one artist's work from beginning to end. You may compare this to the distinctive handwriting or the special tone of voice that are characteristic of individuals throughout their lives. We like to be able to recognize the style of a painter, and find it easiest of course where style is most pronounced, as in the work of El Greco or Van Gogh.

We need a more general background to recognize the ways in which an artist gives expression to the time and place in which he lives, to see how an artist's work fits into the style of his period and his country. He may express the general ideas of his time, he may look backward and sum up what has gone before, or he may look forward and so seem strange and difficult to his contemporaries.

Everything you can learn about history and religion, about literature and music will contribute to an understanding of the way people lived and thought and felt in other times: in eighteenth-century France, for instance, or seventeenth-century Holland, or Renaissance Florence. And this knowledge can help you understand and appreciate the artists who lived and worked during these periods.

The teen-ager who once remarked to me while looking at a slide of Leonardo da Vinci's "Last Supper," "What is this—it seems to be some sort of a bachelor party?" must have been completely insensitive to the atmosphere of the painting itself; unfortunately, her limited experience and knowledge provided no clue to the meaning of a masterpiece of Christian art. The four-year old who examined Masaccio's "Adam and Eve Cast Out of Paradise" and said "Ugh! What did *they* do?" was more discerning.

It is only by knowing something about the seventeenth century in which Rembrandt lived (1606–1669) and about his country, Holland, that we can recognize the greatness and originality of Rembrandt the man. His work might fascinate us, but we would not realize how much Rembrandt created that had never been expressed before in just this way, so moving, so human, so luminous that the drawings and paintings still speak to us directly today, across three hundred years.

Naturally, no one can expect to grasp without effort and study the inner meaning of works of art that deal with mythology or religion, or that give expression to the life of a people. For some of the masterpieces of Buddhist and Hindu art we need an open mind and as much knowledge of the culture as we can absorb. The four arms of the great god Shiva, Lord of the Dance, were as natural, as vivid a symbol to people of Hindu faith in medieval India as were the wings of the Angel Gabriel to Christians in medieval Europe. Study in turn sends us back to the works of art with more perceptive questions, with more ability to sense what the artists are saying through the language of line, color, and form. For not everything that is thought and felt by human beings will fit into verbal patterns; music and art are other languages, capable of shades of feeling, of nuances that may slip through the web of words.

South Indian, eleventh century SHIVA NATARAJA

5

Why Is the New Always Difficult?

About a hundred years ago the French painter Edouard Manet began to rethink the long-accepted convention of painting forms or volumes by modeling with light and shade (a technique known as *chiaroscuro*). He was convinced that this was not the way we really see the world, especially figures and faces seen out of doors. So when he painted "The Fifer," he broke with a tradition that goes all the way back to the Renaissance painter Leonardo da Vinci and even earlier. You can see how the picture is built up in rather flat tones. You can see this in the face of the boy; you can see also that no distinction is made between the ground and distance, or perhaps it is floor and wall. When Manet painted the "Luncheon on the Grass" it was not only the nude lady at a picnic who caused the scandal, it was a new way of seeing that upset people, the flat lighting without the familiar modeling of forms from light into a rather colorless shadow (see page 45).

The way was open to new ways of seeing. Another French painter, Claude Monet, began to break up the shadows as well as the sunlight into short, choppy strokes of juxtaposed color that brought a new lightness and sparkle into painting. But newspaper critics and angry crowds attacked what seemed to them the destruction of all they had admired in painting. The new was too difficult for them to accept.

A critic, seizing on the title of a painting by Monet, "Impression: Sunrise," gave the name Impressionism in scorn to the group of painters working and exhibiting together in the 1870's and 1880's. Monet, Camille Pissarro, Renoir, sometimes Manet and Edgar Degas, with Berthe Morisot, Alfred Sisley, and the American Mary Cassatt are among the artists associated with Impressionism.

Now after two world wars we look back at the gay and charming world of Monet and Renoir and their friends and wonder how their paintings could have shocked anyone and why these devoted and perservering artists, the Impressionists, had to live through such hard years of struggle before the public began to catch up with them.

Cézanne, Van Gogh, and Paul Gauguin are usually called Post-Impressionists. Each of them brought a new interpretation to the Impressionist use of color: Cézanne in his lonely pursuit of formal order, Gauguin with his symbolic and decorative color (best known to us in the South Seas paintings), and Van Gogh with his emotional and expressive color. Each of these three painters pursued his own vision in the face of great difficulties, almost insurmountable material difficulties for Van Gogh and Gauguin.

At the time Van Gogh died no one wanted to buy his paintings. Only his brother Theo and one or two loyal friends believed in him as a serious, creative artist. To the average taste of his time, Vincent van Gogh's paintings were rough, wild, unfinished, and showed an unbalanced mind. You have only to look at the painting by Gérôme to see what most people expected toward the end of the last century. They admired what they considered accomplished drawing, and a finished technique in oil colors. They liked pretty and pleasant subjects: girls in white dresses or no dresses at all, and scenes of luxury in Oriental courts. Obviously Van Gogh's painting was not what they expected and so they rejected it. Vincent van Gogh's troubled and searching and deeply poetic mind could not accept the obviously superficial.

Léon Gérôme PYGMALION AND GALATEA   *Edouard Manet* LUNCHEON ON THE GRASS

In one of his letters to his brother, he wrote:

> So I am always between two currents of thought, first the material difficulties, turning round and round to make a living; and second, study of color. I am always in hope of making a discovery there, to express the love of two lovers by a wedding of two complementary colors, their mingling and their opposition, the mysterious vibrations of kindred tones. To express the thought of a brow by the radiance of a light tone against a somber background.
>
> To express hope by some star, the eagerness of a soul by a sunset radiance. Certainly there is no delusive realism in that, but isn't it something that actually exists?[1]

Along about 1908 came another major direction in painting called Cubism, in which the real world of figures or guitars or bowls of fruit and pipes seems to disappear entirely into tilting planes and shifting space in low-keyed color; this is a way of painting which has taken its place firmly in the long tradition of Western art. Pablo Picasso, Georges Braque, and Juan Gris are the most important artists associated with the innovations of this style.

Again, after the upheaval of World War II, a group of artists in New York felt that it was impossible to go on in the established paths. They wanted to make a new beginning, to start with the very most deeply felt

Willem de Kooning FIGURE

and intuitive meanings in painting. These Abstract Expressionist painters of New York—Jackson Pollock, Willem de Kooning, Franz Kline, and others—gave to this country our first truly original and influential style of painting.

You may ask why art cannot continue repeating itself, why there are always artists with new ways of seeing and doing. It is partly because a certain vein comes to be exhausted. What once was fresh and stimulating and full of meaning in the hands of strong and original painters becomes stale and repetitious in the hands of later imitators. Also the attitudes and interests of society as a whole shift and change, and it is the artists and the scientists who are often the first to provide intimations of this change. Just as people are beginning to grow accustomed to the artists' ways of seeing, a new generation of painters comes along to upset the familiar vision, and change is difficult for the majority of people.

In our own time, in this second half of the twentieth century, there is no such clearly defined opposition between conventional taste and advanced art as there was a hundred years ago when Edouard Manet and Claude Monet began to paint. There are instead many styles, many ways of seeing and working, and they involve artists all over the world. We seem to have what may be called "instant art." What is new in New York or Paris appears simultaneously in San Francisco or Tokyo or Buenos Aires or London. Sometimes catchwords like "pop" (or popular) art and "op" (or optical) art confuse the public by lumping together artists who work in the

Edwin Mieczkowski WAVERLY PLACE

Roy Lichtenstein PORTRAIT OF HOLLY

Frank Gallo MALE IMAGE

same general manner, without distinguishing the serious artists from those who are trying to climb on the bandwagon.

Some people are afraid of missing anything that might possibly become important, and therefore accept everything without discrimination. Others shut their eyes to everything that has happened in the arts in the last half century. But for those with an open mind it is an adventurous time to be young and an artist, or collector, a student of art history, or just an interested observer.

In Dag Hammarskjöld's words:

> All first-hand experience is valuable, and he who has given up looking for it will one day find—that he lacks what he needs: a closed mind is a weakness, and he who approaches persons or painting or poetry without the youthful ambition to learn a new language and so gain access to someone else's perspective on life, let him beware.[2]

Interlude: A Collage of
Pictures and Quotations

Seeing the immense design of the world, one image of wonder mirrored by another image of wonder—the pattern of fern and of feather by the frost on the window-pane, the six rays of the snowflake mirrored in the rock-crystal's six-rayed eternity—seeing the pattern on the scaly legs of birds mirrored in the pattern of knot-grass, I asked myself, were those shapes molded by blindness? Are not these the "correspondences," to quote a phrase of Swedenborg, "whereby we may speak with angels"?

—*Edith Sitwell*

FERN IN RAIN, MOUNT RAINIER NATIONAL PARK
Photograph by Ansel Adams

from

Lapis Lazuli

———

Two Chinamen, behind them a third,
Are carved in lapis lazuli,
Over them flies a long-legged bird,
A symbol of longevity;
The third, doubtless a serving-man,
Carries a musical instrument.

Every discoloration of the stone,
Every accidental crack or dent,
Seems a water-course or an avalanche,
Or lofty slope where it still snows
Though doubtless plum or cherry-branch
Sweetens the little half-way house
Those Chinamen climb towards, and I
Delight to imagine them seated there;
There, on the mountain and the sky,
On all the tragic scene they stare.
One asks for mournful melodies;
Accomplished fingers begin to play.
Their eyes mid many wrinkles, their eyes,
Their ancient, glittering eyes, are gay.

—William Butler Yeats

Wu Pin GREETING THE SPRING (detail)

American, nineteenth century BABY IN A RED CHAIR

On the Birth of His Son

Families, when a child is born
Want it to be intelligent.
I, through intelligence,
Having wrecked my whole life,
Only hope the baby will prove
Ignorant and stupid.
Then he will crown a tranquil life
By becoming a Cabinet Minister.

—*Su Tung-p'o (1036–1101)*

Pablo Picasso   THE OLD GUITARIST

from
The Man With the Blue Guitar

The man bent over his blue guitar
A shearsman of sorts. The day was green.

They said, "You have a blue guitar,
You do not play things as they are."

The man replied, "Things as they are
Are changed upon the blue guitar."

And they said then, "But play, you must,
A tune beyond us, yet ourselves,

A tune upon the blue guitar
Of things exactly as they are."

—*Wallace Stevens*

Stopping by Woods on a Snowy Evening

Whose woods these are I think I know.
His house is in the village though;
He will not see me stopping here
To watch his woods fill up with snow.

My little horse must think it queer
To stop without a farmhouse near
Between the woods and frozen lake
The darkest evening of the year.

He gives his harness bells a shake
To ask if there is some mistake.
The only other sound's the sweep
Of easy wind and downy flake.

The woods are lovely, dark and deep,
But I have promises to keep,
And miles to go before I sleep,
And miles to go before I sleep.

—Robert Frost

Not a shelter to stop the steed
In the snowy dusk at Sano no Watari

—Fujiwara Teika

Sotatsu   CROSSING AT SANO (SANO NO WATARI)

The Hunters in the Snow

The over-all picture is winter
icy mountains
in the background the return

from the hunt it is toward evening
from the left
sturdy hunters lead in

their pack the inn-sign
hanging from a
broken hinge is a stag a crucifix

between his antlers the cold
inn yard is
deserted but for a huge bonfire

that flares wind-driven tended by
women who cluster
about it to the right beyond

the hill is a pattern of skaters
Brueghel the painter
concerned with it all has chosen

a winter-struck bush for his
foreground to
complete the picture . . .

—William Carlos Williams

Pieter Brueghel   HUNTERS IN THE SNOW

Only through art can we get outside of ourselves and know another's view of the universe which is not the same as ours and see landscapes which would otherwise have remained unknown to us like the landscapes on the moon. Thanks to art, instead of seeing a single world, our own, we see it multiply until we have before us as many worlds as there are original artists—more different from each other than those which revolve in space. And many centuries after their core, whether we call it Rembrandt or Vermeer, is extinguished they continue to send us their special rays.

—*Marcel Proust*

Rembrandt van Rijn THE ARTIST IN HIS STUDIO

Jan Vermeer THE ARTIST IN HIS STUDIO

"We practice," wrote Nicolas Poussin, "a silent art." In this silent Dutch painting the eye is led from room to room by an extraordinary handling of light and space. The eye is also led, by some uncanny leap of the artist's imagination, into seeing hints of twentieth-century ideas in painting. Compare a section of the floor with the Mondrian. Notice the reflection in the mirror, which suggests the compositions of Pierre Bonnard.

Emanuel de Witte INTERIOR WITH A HARPSICHORD

(Opposite) *Piet Mondrian* PAINTING NO. I

Before seeing Chardin's pictures, I never realized how much beauty there was around me in my parents' home, in the half-cleared table, the lifted corner of a table cloth, a knife beside the oyster shell.

—*Marcel Proust*

To make a still-life, a painter and an apple must reciprocally confront and correct each other. And if the forms are nothing without the light of this world, they also contribute their own luminosity to that light.

—*Albert Camus*

Jean Simeon Chardin THE SKATE

Paul Cézanne STILL LIFE WITH APPLES

Paul Gauguin THE HOUSE OF THE MAORI

Sir Kenneth Clark, in his book *Landscape into Painting*, points out that Gauguin had to take an immense journey in space in order to achieve a journey in time, and that the landscapes painted in Tahiti are the true successors to the tapestry landscapes of the fourteenth century.

Arras Tapestry   SCENE FROM A NOVEL

Sailing to Byzantium

That is no country for old men. The young
In one another's arms, birds in the trees,
—Those dying generations—at their song,
The salmon-falls, the mackerel-crowded seas,
Fish, flesh, or fowl, commend all summer long
Whatever is begotten, born, and dies
Caught in that sensual music all neglect
Monuments of unageing intellect.

An aged man is but a paltry thing,
A tattered coat upon a stick, unless
Soul clap its hands and sing, and louder sing
For every tatter in its mortal dress,
Nor is there singing school but studying
Monuments of its own magnificence;
And therefore I have sailed the seas and come
To the holy city of Byzantium.

THE HOLY VIRGINS (mosaic)

O sages standing in God's holy fire
As in the gold mosaic of a wall,
Come from the holy fire, perne in a gyre,
And be the singing-masters of my soul.
Consume my heart away; sick with desire
And fastened to a dying animal
It knows not what it is; and gather me
Into the artifice of eternity.

Once out of nature I shall never take
My bodily form from any natural thing,
But such a form as Grecian goldsmiths make
Of hammered gold and gold enamelling
To keep a drowsy Emperor awake;
Or set upon a golden bough to sing
To lords and ladies of Byzantium
Of what is past, or passing, or to come.

—*William Butler Yeats*

THE HOLY MARTYRS (mosaic)

Kitagawa Utamaro   ONE OF THE SEVEN WOMEN SEEN IN A MIRROR

Pablo Picasso   GIRL BEFORE A MIRROR

On Hearing Chün the Buddhist Monk From Shu Play His Lute

The monk from Shu with his
    green silk lute-case,
Walking west down O'mêi Mountain,
Has brought me by one touch
    of the strings
The breath of pines in a
    thousand valleys.
I hear him in the cleansing brook,
I hear him in the icy bells;
And I feel no change though
    the mountain darkens
And cloudy autumn heaps the sky.

                    —*Li Po (701–762)*

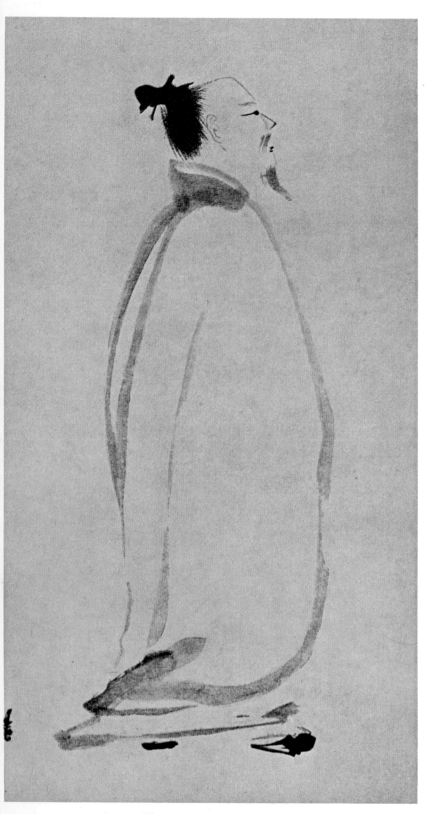

Liang K'ai LI PO CHANTING A POEM

6

The Seeing Eye, the Thinking Hand

It is your turn now to take up a pencil and draw, to pick up a brush and paint, if only to investigate the meaning of the words and phrases we have been using in this book. You will not find out from this book how to become an artist in six easy lessons, or how to make an oil painting. There are no paint-by-number picture puzzles. Instead, you will follow a series of exercises or investigations that are planned to give you a feeling for simple tools and materials. You will be able to explore for yourself, and in a non-verbal way, the meaning of such words as line, color, form, texture and pattern, composition, rhythm, balance, energy, relaxation, open, contained. If this interests you, you will go on to invent exercises for yourself. Keep what you do for a while at least and see whether there is any apparent direction or development in what you are doing.

DRAWING

"I make a head to see how I see, to know how I see, not to make a work of art." The Swiss sculptor and painter Alberto Giacometti said that. Drawing, then, is really a way of perceiving, a kind of thinking. You yourself will probably never see the shape of a leaf, a bone, a shell more clearly than when you are drawing. The effort to set down shape, texture, and structure makes, I always imagine, a little track in the brain, it leaves a mark like that made by a needle cutting a record, long after the drawing is forgotten. For this kind of drawing, observation and concentration are required; the mind must be in the tip of the pencil.

For drawing, use a soft pencil, a 4 B or an Ebony pencil, a fountain pen, a Chinese brush, or a stick dipped in India ink. Play a little with the tool before you begin, like a pianist running his fingers over the keyboard or like tennis players exchanging a few shots before the game begins. See if you can hold a pencil or pen in some position other than the way you ordinarily hold it for writing. It will feel awkward at first but will move more freely from the wrist and the whole arm.

Sometimes try to draw with your eye resting only on the object—a leaf, a stone, a flower—your hand, moving in a continuous line, steadily expressing just the outer contours. The hand should respond sensitively to every variation of form or direction, even of texture; never lift the pencil, never look down at the paper. (A very sharp pencil, a fountain pen, or a steel pen provide the most responsive line.) Never mind how distorted the drawing is. It is the looking that is important. Get someone to pose for you. Take your courage in your hand and draw, in the same way, a head or the whole figure.

Drawing can be approached from two opposing points of view. For the intuitive way, you will launch out into space with conviction, daring yourself to do it, pulling something out of the mess of scribbles that search for directions. Forget about erasers; work directly, developing your drawing from the first rough scribbles. This bold attack has to be disciplined by the second kind of drawing—thoughtful, analytical, constructive. Some knowledge of perspective, among other things, comes under this heading. For this second way, you will eventually want experienced and competent instruction.

Regardless of how you draw, the boundaries of your paper can help you. I once heard a singer speak of the idea that the four walls of a room held her voice, sustained it within a framework. And in the same way that the four sides of your paper can help you contain your drawing, a block of marble limits and contains a sculpture.

CONSTRUCTION

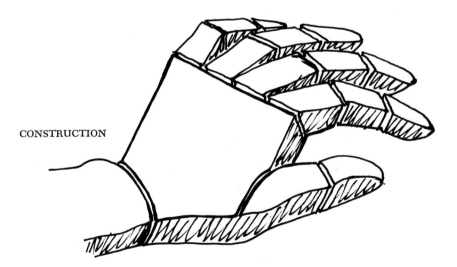

Composition, the aim of which is expression, alters itself according to the surface to be covered. If I take a sheet of paper of given dimensions I will jot down a drawing which will have a necessary relation to its format—I will not repeat this drawing on another sheet of different dimensions, for instance on a rectangular sheet if the first one happened to be square.

—Henri Matisse[1]

One Square Foot of Earth. Take a large paper, 14″ x 17″ or 18″ x 24″, and sit down in the long grass. Choose about one square foot of earth and draw the grass, twigs, and weeds enlarged many times. Using a pen, brush, or felt-tipped pen, completely fill your page with the forms that you see. Judge your own drawing for observation, concentration, composition, variety and character of line, and textures.

TEXTURES AND PATTERNS

Have you a scrap of fur, a few grains of rice, a section of lemon, the bark of a tree, moss, stones, ferns? Look at them under a magnifying glass and you will realize the variety that is all around us. If you look intently enough, with a kind of hypnotic fascination, you can invent small patches of pattern and texture and provide yourself with an infinite variety of exercises and investigations. You can invent equivalents for this variety, using just a few simple tools: pen and ink, water and a brush, or a pencil, or a black and a white crayon.

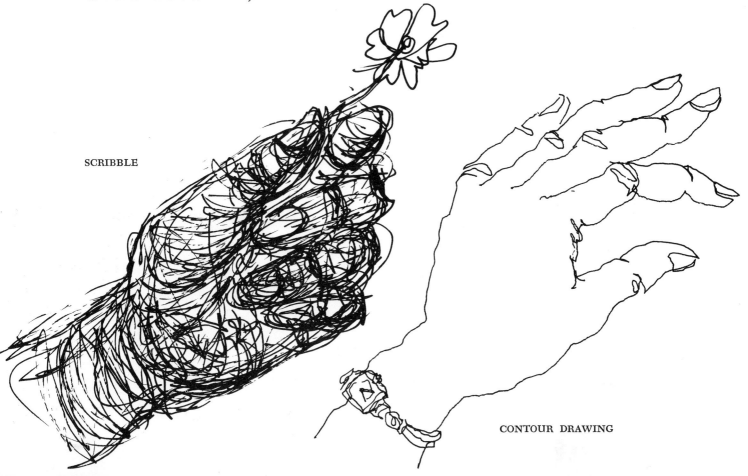

SCRIBBLE

CONTOUR DRAWING

COMPOSITION

Rule a sheet with a half a dozen 4″ x 6″ rectangles or take some 4″ x 6″ unruled file cards. Start with your pencil or fine-tipped felt pen in the upper left-hand corner. "Take a walk with a line." Let your hand move evenly, not jerkily, in and out and roundabout this area, crossing over and under and eventually returning to your starting point. Make some compositions that are tangled and thick, the line touching the outside edges of the frame from time to time; make others with large slow curves, some with straight lines and angles, but always a continuous line returning to the starting point, a line that has "derivation and destination."

Now, choose one of these line drawings and select out of the tangle of irregular shapes made by the intersecting lines a single shape to shade in with an even, dark tone. You will now have both shape and line or, we may say, figure and ground. Try this again and again until you have a satisfying balance of line and shape. Then try selecting not one but two shapes, a larger and a smaller one, keeping a sense of balance in your small composition.

Cut a 2¼″ x 3″ window in a sheet of 8½″ x 11″ paper. Choose one of the reproductions in this book and move your window slowly over the surface, disregarding subject matter, until you have isolated a small area that pleases you. Does it interest you as linear movement, or as light and dark values? As color relations, or as formal order or design? This exercise can help you see that in the old master paintings there are no dead areas. The outer edges of the paintings often have their own kind of interest.

Take your window and move it over the pages of photography or advertising in any magazines you have handy. Choose a dozen interesting small areas. Cut them out and paste them down on your file cards. Decide why you have chosen them. Is it because of light and dark contrast? Pattern? Texture? Color harmony or dissonance? Rhythmic movement?

LINES, SHAPES, PATTERNS

In small patches, practice a few patterns; the Greek vase painting on page 105 will give you some suggestions. Returning now to your 4″ x 6″ frames or file cards, cut out of a colored or toned paper any two of these three geometric shapes: a square, a triangle, a circle. Paste them down to make a thoughtful composition. Then add for pleasure and liveliness a few patterns—not more than two or three—to give sparkle to the whole surface.

You can also discover patterns and textures by stamping with bits of sponge, with the end of a spool dipped in watercolor or ink, or with an eraser or with a cross-section of potato as a stamp. You can make rubbings by placing a piece of lightweight paper over a patterned object—coins, rubber mats, concrete surfaces, manhole covers, tree bark—and then rubbing over the surface with a soft pencil. Save your experiments. They can be useful in collages.

COLOR

Once I heard a small boy say, as he painted a great swatch of blue, "I am going to play a joke on my blue, I am going to put some red in it." The following suggestions are all on the side of play, fantasy, intuition, experiment.

Again rule small rectangles or use the 4″ x 6″ file cards. All you need are a child's box of crayons and a little watercolor box which usually comes with a pointed brush. You will also like using a square-tipped brush if you can get one. Set yourself the task of filling the frames with color in as many and as varied ways as you can invent. It may help you to work in pairs:

> bright and dark
> cool and warm
> delicate and strong
> formal and capricious
> optimistic and gloomy
> wet washes and controlled areas

or you may try using complementary colors:

> a red composition with green accents
> a green composition with red accents
> an orange composition with blue accents
> a blue composition with orange accents
> a yellow composition with violet accents
> a violet composition with yellow accents

Look out a window and make color notes about the relations of color that you see, ignoring the problem of drawing the shapes. In this case, city roofs or a parking lot make as useful an exercise as fields or trees.

Illustrate in your own way the following quotation: "Annihilating all that's made to a green thought in a green shade" (Andrew Marvell).

78

In one of his letters Van Gogh wrote about the artist Vermeer who painted a beautiful Dutch lady, Van Gogh said, with a palette made up of blue, lemon yellow, pearly gray, black, and white. Van Gogh observed that with these limited colors Vermeer's picture seemed to have all the richness of a full palette.

On a small paper, make a nonrepresentational painting, similar to those in your series above, using only blue, yellow, gray, black, and various whites. Turn your paper so that the composition may be seen from any angle.

"Watercolor Chess" is a game that requires a partner and at least as much concentration as a game of ordinary chess. Lay out a small rectangle. Have ready a box of watercolors, pen and ink, a crayon or two. You may take the first turn. Choose any of the materials and make "one move," one splash, stroke, line, or area of color within the frame. (Work with shapes, colors, or patterns, not with pictures of anything.) Your partner adds a counterbalancing stroke, splash, or area. He may even make the colors of his "move" cross over or run into your first stroke. When it is your turn again, proceed thoughtfully to add whatever you feel is called for by what has already been set down. Turn the paper from time to time so that the composition is equally interesting from all sides. When you lay down your brush, your partner has the next move. This game has to be played quietly, slowly, thoughtfully. By common agreement you stop when, we hope, you are both still ahead.

COLLAGE

Collage is simply the French word for something pasted. The Cubist painters, especially Braque and Picasso, made use of pasted paper (*papiers collés*), sometimes of newspaper, music sheets, wallpaper, and advertising, to bring an element of surprise, of a real, flat surface into the pictorial space of their compositions. The advantage for an amateur of working with cut or torn paper is that he is forced to a decision. There are no blurred edges as in watercolor. Collect pages from old magazines, bits of printed paper, colored tissues, discarded exercises from the series in this book, and keep them all in a box ready to be cut up, torn, and pasted into small studies. Library paste, rubber cement, or Elmer's glue can be used as adhesive. For collages using tissues, Elmer's glue, diluted with water to the consistency of cream and applied with a brush, is very satisfactory. Overlapping colored tissues suggest many interesting color projects.

Robert Motherwell MALLARMÉ'S SWAN

Many of the exercises suggested under Drawing, Composition, and Color can also be done with collage materials. You can add string, thread, bark, and other materials, but be careful to use them with restraint or you will have a jumble. On the other hand, a bold and convincing enough jumble can be dignified with the title of "assemblage," which is a sort of three-dimensional collage.

I know a family that held a competition in their front yard for the best assemblage made from "found objects"—discarded furniture, household utensils, toys, scraps of wood, branches, or dried grasses—fastened or glued together in sculptured forms. There was a prize for each member of the family and each guest: the most delicate, the most daring, the most abstract, the most witty, the biggest, the smallest, and so on.

SOME MORE ADVANCED PROJECTS

The Bouquet of Flowers

Find an old seed catalogue and cut out a picture of a single flower. Paste it down toward the center of a large sheet of paper. With poster paints or

80

watercolors or crayons (or all three) paint many flower shapes all around it; invent a whole bouquet (flowers first, stems and leaves only after you have a fine clutter of flowers). See if you can make the bouquet so lively, so vivid, that the eye is distracted and cannot find the one cut-paper, real seed-catalogue flower. You may want to add a basket or a bowl to hold the flowers.

The Calligraphic Landscape

A fine-pointed felt pen is a good tool for this exercise. Begin with some experiments. Write your own name over and over in a free interlocking scribble, your first name, your last name, both names. See what rhythms and repetitions of shape emerge. Make many patches until you begin to see patterns as leaves, bushes, grass, rooftops, or any other features of a landscape. Use other names or words if you like, but not too many. Much of the effect comes from repetition and purposeful but careless energy. Now on a larger sheet, 14" x 17" or 18" x 24", begin improvising trees, bushes, houses, hills, whatever suggests itself as you proceed. Start with the handwritten or "calligraphic" patches that make trees and unify the whole composition with as few extra strokes as possible. Remember the various shapes of familiar trees—wine-glass elms, tall narrow poplars, wide-spreading oaks, or the evergreens.

You may have to make many experiments before you arrive at anything you really like. Overlays of tissue might be a further step.

In many museums it is not necessary to ask permission for sketching provided you are using only a pencil and small sketchbook. It is always wise to inquire, however, since some museums and galleries do not permit sketching certain works.

Collage. This collage of a Chinese owl was made on a sheet 18″ x 24″ by a student in a museum class. She began by filling smaller sheets of white

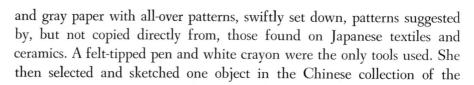

and gray paper with all-over patterns, swiftly set down, patterns suggested by, but not copied directly from, those found on Japanese textiles and ceramics. A felt-tipped pen and white crayon were the only tools used. She then selected and sketched one object in the Chinese collection of the museum, an ancient bronze owl. The idea then was to cut and paste the owl out of the patterns already made and to set the owl into a composition of real leaves observed in another part of the museum. The result is not a literal study of the Chinese owl, but a lively composition based on three different sources: patterns unrelated to the bronze owl, the shape and stance of the owl, the positive and negative shapes of leaves.

This owl collage is but one example from a thousand possibilities offered to an alert and observing eye.

Drawing with both hands at once. This exercise is based on sketches made in the galleries of fairly simple and symmetrical objects. A pencil drawing and some intensive looking should enable you to go home and make a new, bold drawing with both hands at once, a different color felt-

tipped pen in each hand. Using the two colors suggests light and shade and three-dimensional form. Practice at home on a two-handled pot or on the portrait of a friend, preferably one whose hair is parted in the middle and who has two ears showing.

The point of this exercise is to make both hands more courageous and to practice observation and co-ordination.

Assemblage. This is a miniature assemblage put together in a clean sardine tin. The small king and queen were suggested by studies made in a gallery of medieval art where objects of gold, ivory, enamel, and crystal were exhibited. Although nothing is literally copied, the little composition suggests the reflected lights and the richness and sparkle of those precious objects.

The exercises outlined in this chapter assume that the reader has had very little experience in drawing, painting, and design. They are meant to suggest the interaction between the ideas in the mind of an artist and the materials that he selects.

The patient, craftsmanlike skills of the painter working with egg tempera and gold leaf on a gesso panel were appropriate to the medieval artists. They had all the time in the world in which to praise the Lord. The free-flowing, generous brushstrokes possible in oil colors, and the great scale of large canvases were appropriate to master painters like Titian and Rubens, who were equally capable of carrying out commissions for impatient kings and princes, or the splendid large-scale decoration of churches.

You will find out that drawings made with a pen, a broad chalk, or a Chinese brush even when they are similar in subject matter will each have an entirely different and individual character. Through long experience an artist comes to understand the logic of his material. The final work can be described as the result of a continuing dialogue between the artist and his materials.

THE PHOTOGRAPHER'S EYE

One of the best ways to sharpen your own seeing is to use a camera in familiar surroundings. You will find out what an alert and observing eye can discover. You may be able to make photographs that will be what some-one has called "a celebration of the ordinary." This will require not only as much concentration as drawing or painting, but also a certain

(Above) BOY BEHIND STAIRCASE
(Left) GRAND PIANO
Photographs by John Geoghegan, age seventeen

openness and receptiveness. An unboring photograph will never be an exact repetition of what someone else has seen. We may paraphrase Robert Frost's comment, "no surprise for the writer, no surprise for the reader," to say, "no surprise for the photographer, no surprise for the viewer." Remember too that what you actually see within the rectangular viewfinder will be your photograph, not any generalized impression of your surroundings. It is helpful to form the habit of looking through the camera's eye, both literally and figuratively. The mechanics of your camera, the skills of developing, printing, and enlarging, are all important. But the photographer's way of seeing, thinking, and feeling is more important than any of these.

POND AT DAWN *Photograph by John Inglis, age sixteen.* A group of students in an English class who had been reading Thoreau's *Walden* decided to watch the dawn across their local pond. Some were simply observing, some were taking notes, one used a camera. This sensitive photograph stands midway in a sequence of six prints that record the approach of daylight.

7

The Amateur Artist and
the Collector

Amateur musicians probably make the best audience for a concert of classical music. They watch and listen with alert minds to see how the professionals perform, to judge the skill of the musicians, and to become familiar with a variety of musical compositions. Amateur artists ought to be equally perceptive in their field, but this is not always the case. One of the most celebrated amateurs in our century, Sir Winston Churchill, in a little book called *Painting as a Pastime,* speaks in resounding phrases of the resource and pleasure that painting was for him.

> Happy are the painters, for they shall not be lonely. Light and colour, peace and hope, will keep them company to the end, or almost to the end, of the day. . . .
>
> The truth and beauty of line and form which by the slightest touch or twist of the brush a real artist imparts to every feature of his design must be founded on long, hard, persevering apprenticeship and a practice so habitual that it has become instinctive. We must not be too ambitious. We cannot aspire to masterpieces. We may content ourselves with a joyride in a paint box. And for this Audacity is the only ticket.[1]

The most distinguished amateurs in the history of art were undoubtedly the Chinese scholars and poets who were also painters. Sometimes, like Sir Winston Churchill, they were public officials as well. Professional artists have existed for centuries in China, but during certain periods the most brilliant, the most gifted, the most famous artists never accepted money for their ink paintings; they exchanged their paintings with friends or gave them away; they were true amateurs. Painting and writing in China make use of the same tools—ink, brush, and paper or silk. To write the Chinese characters is in itself an exercise in line and form, in rhythm and balance. So anyone who practices the art of handwriting, which is called calligraphy, is well on the way to becoming a painter. Probably the most fascinating paintings for us are the long horizontal landscapes, mounted as scrolls to be unrolled from the right toward the left and enjoyed as if one were taking an imaginary journey through valleys, around coves, over bridges and mountain paths.

We can learn something from these gentlemen-amateurs of China. We can learn that elaborate equipment is not necessary for painting, that a few brushes, ink, and some tubes of watercolor are sufficient. We can learn to look at nature more sympathetically, both the great mountains and the smallest birds, fishes, and insects. We can learn to look at drawings and paintings of earlier times with more appreciation, and we can plan some-day to own a modest collection of drawings or original prints so as to train our own eyes for further ventures.

Some of the great and serious collectors of art in our time started when they were young. Mrs. Horace O. Havemeyer, with her husband, left a splendid collection of paintings to the Metropolitan Museum in New York. She began collecting as a schoolgirl in Paris when her friend, a young

Shih-t'ao SPRING ON THE MIN RIVER

American artist named Mary Cassatt, persuaded her to spend her allowance for small paintings they saw in shop windows. That is the way Mrs. Havemeyer came to know the work of Monet and Renoir and Degas and began to acquire their work when the painters were also young and unknown.

Perhaps you cannot yet venture into buying small works of art. But you can still collect stones for their shape and color, or shells, grasses, seaweed, mosses. Color harmonies, stray ideas for paintings or collages may be suggested, even ideas for color in the house or for dress. Or you can collect postage stamps for their fine design. A collection of the world's most beautiful postage stamps carefully mounted would be a collection of miniature engravings.

You have probably heard people say, "I can't draw a straight line, but I know what I like." You might reply, "I can draw a straight line very easily, with a ruler, but I don't know what I like—yet." It takes looking at many kinds of art to find out what you like, training your eyes in museums and galleries, and in artists' studios, if such places are accessible to you, or by looking thoughtfully at books and reproductions. Then if you can also refresh your eyes by looking at the world of nature—at rocks and trees and grasses, at fields and hills, and at the sky and water, you will begin to find out what your own preferences are, to form your own taste, a taste that can change and grow your whole life long.

Honoré Daumier CONNOISSEURS

8

Materials and Techniques
of the Artist

The amateur artist, the collector, and the student all need to know something about materials and techniques for their own understanding and enjoyment. The character of an artist's work is determined, in part, by the range and limitation of his materials. Often the artist learns to make the most out of limited means. He may develop new materials in response to the demands of patrons, of architects, of the society in which he lives. In this chapter you will find a brief discussion of the materials most commonly used in drawing, painting, sculpture, and printmaking.

DRAWING

When we think about drawings we usually think of those made with pen and ink, with brush and ink, or with pencil or charcoal. Medieval artists drew on parchment (usually sheepskin) or on vellum (calfskin) with quill or reed pens. Inks were variously made, sometimes simply by grinding carbon with water. Artists of the early Renaissance made beautiful, delicate drawings with a metal point on a paper prepared with a size, usually glue and pigment. The prepared papers were often colored blue, gray, rose, or green. A silverpoint line shows on this surface because the silver tip oxidizes a path across the prepared paper. (You can experiment by painting a patch of casein white on paper or cardboard and marking on it with the edge of a silver dime or with silver wire inserted in a mechanical pencil.)

Later artists preferred a broader, freer method of drawing and turned to pen and ink with washes, or to chalks, pastels, and crayons.

Chalks, pastels, and crayons can produce broad strokes. Each stroke leaves behind a track of crumbled material that forms the line. Chalks may

90

1. *Jean Auguste Dominique Ingres*   PORTRAIT OF MADAME RAOUL-ROCHETTE
2. *Pablo Picasso*   RECLINING NUDE
3. *Jean Antoine Watteau*   STUDY FOR THE ROMANCER
4. *Ernest Ludwig Kirchner*   MOUNTAIN LANDSCAPE WITH FIR TREES
5. *Giovanni Domenico Tiepolo*   THE SPRING SHOWER

1. Pencil

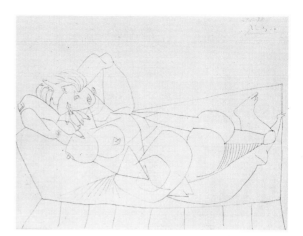

2. Pen line

3. Red and black chalk

DRAWING TECHNIQUES

4. Pencil and brush and India ink

5. Pen and bistre ink and
bistre wash

be natural (small chunks from the white cliffs of England, for example, or bits of red or gray chalk). Those we buy are made of powdered pigments held together with a binder. In the case of crayons the binder has an oily or waxy quality.

Charcoal may be simply a burned twig, but in modern manufacture it is more likely to be made of compressed particles of carbon. Graphite, like chalk, was originally found as a deposit in the earth, but as we know it now in wooden pencils it is chemically produced, and the relative hardness or softness is controlled in manufacture.

PAINTING

Watercolor

Watercolor is pigment mixed with gum arabic; it is soluble in water, which evaporates when the paint layer is applied to paper or silk. Watercolor was widely used in the Middle Ages, in the Near East and the Far East. We speak of transparent watercolors in which the whiteness of the paper shines through thin washes of color, and of opaque watercolor in which the pigment is usually mixed with some opaque white so that the paper does not show through the color. A particular kind of opaque watercolor is called "gouache." Most of Chinese and Japanese painting is made either with ink or with ink and watercolor on paper or silk. In the West, some of the most effective watercolors were made by nineteenth-century English artists. J. M. W. Turner is an outstanding example.

Fresco

Fresco is a technique for painting on plaster walls. In true fresco the paint is applied to wet plaster so that the colors are chemically locked into the plaster as it dries. By the fourteenth century, Italian artists were highly skilled in this art, which requires careful planning, speed, and assurance on the part of the artist, along with an understanding of how to work with limited colors. Once the plaster has set, alterations and corrections cannot be made. Giotto's frescoes in the Arena Chapel at Padua (1305–1306) and Michelangelo's ceiling of the Sistine Chapel (1534–1541) are masterpieces in this technique.

Tempera

The term tempera generally means a kind of painting in which egg is used as a medium, usually the yolk of an egg, sometimes the whole egg mixed with a little water. The medium makes it possible to apply pigments to the ground or prepared surface. Altarpieces and panel paintings in Italy in the fourteenth and fifteenth centuries were painted on wood panels prepared with a smooth white gesso surface. The gesso (an Italian word pronounced "jesso") consisted of plaster of Paris dissolved in animal-skin glue and water and was applied with great care in many coats. Tempera painting requires the careful preparation of preliminary drawings and a slow building up the painting. Areas of color stay within clearly defined outlines. The fourteenth- and fifteenth-century painter's knowledge of his craft was so thorough and so sound that many tempera paintings are even now in a better state of preservation than the oil paintings which came later.

Oil

Painters nowadays buy oil colors in tubes; the pigments are commercially ground, mixed with oil, and stored in tubes. Since linen or cotton canvas is rather like blotting paper, the surface is usually coated with a preparation that will make it firmer, less absorbent, and more agreeable to the brush. Some artists stretch their own canvas on wooden stretchers and give it priming coats, sometimes of homemade or commercially prepared gesso, while others buy ready-prepared canvas. Still others prefer to paint on "presdwood panels."* Since our modern oil colors in tubes are rather thick, the artist usually mixes them with a medium before applying them to the canvas; this may be a combination of turpentine and linseed oil, or of turpentine, linseed oil, and varnish. Many kinds of brushes can be used, flat bristle brushes, round bristle brushes, or soft brushes. Sometimes paint is applied with a palette knife, a spray can, or the fingers.

Oil painting was developed in Flanders in the fifteenth century and adopted by Italian painters of the Renaissance. An underpainting in tempera may have been used at first with successive layers of oil paint over it. In the sixteenth century the artists of Venice developed a free and broad way of using oil colors on canvas. Sometimes they worked on a light ground, sometimes on a toned ground, often of a reddish-brown color. On a toned ground, light areas were indicated in white and dark areas in a deeper tone. Thus the painting developed logically from a drawing on the canvas, to a drawing with indications of light, middle, and dark tones, then

*This is a commercially manufactured building board, less subject to cracking than a natural wood panel.

to a washing in or "glazing" of transparent colors, and finally to the use of thick opaque colors in the highlights.

In the nineteenth century, painters more often worked directly, stating the final colors from the start, as in Van Gogh's paintings. In the twentieth century, oil colors have been used with great freedom and much exploitation of chance effects. Oil colors have also been used with geometrical precision. New kinds of paints—polymers and plastics—have also been developed to answer new demands of the painters. Rapid drying and the ability to cover large areas with a mat, flat, unshiny surface are among these requirements.

In a sense our traditional use of oil colors on canvas corresponds to such traditional instruments of the symphony orchestra as the violin, cello, and flute. What the developments of our age of technology will eventually do to musical instruments or to the materials of the artist remains to be seen.

COLLAGE

The term collage may refer to pasted papers, or to a composition in mixed techniques, partly painted, partly pasted. This technique was exploited with great success by Picasso and Braque in their Cubist work. By introducing fragments such as newspaper, advertisements, sheet music, or wallpaper the artist forces the viewer to see these areas as flat shapes, thus creating a tension among the various forms.

PRINTS AND PRINTMAKING

In the vocabulary of the fine arts, the term "prints" refers only to those impressions produced by or under the direct supervision of an artist from his own woodblock, metal plate, or lithographic stone. Each individual impression is numbered and signed by the artist and each one in a series is considered an original work of art. There may be, for example, twenty impressions from one woodblock. They will be similar but not necessarily exactly identical, and they will be numbered from one to twenty. You may find yourself buying 4/20, the fourth print in a series of twenty. Much confusion would be avoided if all commercially printed reproductions of drawings and paintings, made by photomechanical methods, were called reproductions and the term prints were reserved as it should be for "fine prints," which are handmade original works of art.

There are three main kinds of prints: relief, intaglio, and printing from a flat or plane surface (lithography and silk screen).

94

1. *Giovanni Battista Piranesi* THE PRISONS: AN IMMENSE INTERIOR WITH A DRAWBRIDGE
2. *Lyonel Feininger* HOUSES IN OLD PARIS
3. *Eugène Delacroix* WILD HORSE
4. *Israhel van Meckenem* THE ORGAN PLAYER AND HIS WIFE
5. *Rembrandt van Rijn* THE THREE CROSSES (detail)

1. Etching

2. Woodcut

3. Lithograph

4. Engraving

5. Etching and drypoint

Relief

If you have ever cut a linoleum block, inked it, and made prints from it, you will readily understand the term "relief print." The areas to be inked remain at the surface level and all else is cut away, so that only the areas in relief will be printed. A woodcut often has a rather bold, strong, honest look with the tool marks showing how the wood has been cut away, leaving the drawing or design in relief. The block may be printed by laying a damp paper over the inked block and rubbing the back of the paper with a spoon; or it may be printed in a press that comes down from above. You can experiment with relief printing by slicing a potato in half, cutting away certain areas, painting the relief surface with poster paints, watercolor, or colored ink, and stamping impressions on a paper towel. You can also make a relief block by building up a wood or cardboard surface with bits of cardboard, wood, or string dipped in Elmer's glue.

Intaglio

Intaglio is the Italian word for carving or incising. The three most common kinds of intaglio print are engraving, etching, and drypoint.

Engraving, the oldest of the three methods, owes something to the ornamentation of armor worn by medieval knights. A metal tool with a diamond-shaped point is pushed along the polished surface of a copper or zinc plate, which is turned as the line curves. The tool also may dig short flecks and furrows. The whole surface is then inked and wiped clean, leaving ink only in the incised furrows or lines. When damp paper is laid on the plate and then rolled through a heavy press under heavy pressure, the inked lines are transferred to the paper. The result is an engraving, one of a number that can be taken from the same plate. The characteristic of engraving is the clarity and power of the line.

The Italian term for etching describes the process: *intaglio ad aqua forte* (incising with acid). The metal plate, generally copper, is coated with a ground usually made of beeswax and asphaltum. Lines are lightly scratched through this ground without marring the surface of the copper. When the plate is immersed in an acid bath, the action of the acid "bites" or eats away the metal wherever the ground has been opened up, leaving the metal unprotected. A printmaker usually returns his plate to the acid many times, slowly and thoughtfully building up a network of lines that provide a variety of tones from delicate grays to rich blacks when the plate is inked, wiped, and printed between the rollers of the press. Impressions taken at various stages along the way are called proofs or states.

A drypoint print is made by digging along the surface of the polished plate with a steel needle, which raises up a burr or rough edge as it is dragged along the surface. The special quality of a drypoint impression comes from the scratchy edge of the line, which may print as a soft blur since it is liable to hold some of the ink. Rembrandt, the master printmaker, often combined etched and drypoint lines. Contemporary printmakers have experimented in many techniques and combinations of methods.

Lithography

The process of lithography was invented at the end of the eighteenth century in Munich by Aloys Senefelder. It is used both as a method of printmaking by artists and commercially as a means of reproducing drawings. Lithography is based on the idea of drawing with a greasy crayon on a special kind of smooth limestone. The drawing must be "etched" with a solution of gum arabic and acid. The surface of the stone is then moistened with water. The parts covered by the greasy crayon repel the water, the rest remains wet. When oily ink is applied with a roller, the ink sticks to the greasy crayon marks and not to the wet stone. A paper pressed against the stone reproduces the inky lines (in reverse, of course).

Silk-screen Printing

Silk-screen printing is a stencil process which, like lithography, has commercial applications. Printmakers who use this technique call their impressions serigraphs. Like woodblocks and linoleum cuts, silk screen can also be used for printing textiles.

Monotype Prints

In monotype printing, a painting or drawing in oil colors or printer's ink is made, usually on a glass plate. A damp paper is pressed down on the plate, absorbing the color. There is some question whether monotypes should properly be included among print processes, since only one impression can be made from a plate.

SCULPTURE

The two basic methods available to the sculptor are *carving*, or cutting

97

away, and *modeling*, or building up in a plastic material. The process of carving a piece of sculpture has been described in a familiar story about the old man who said that carving was easy: "first you see the bear in the block of wood and then you cut away what isn't bear." Modeling is a different matter. The hands that gather up a lump of wet clay must push and press and build it into the shape of a bear.

Woodcarvers and stonecutters find both challenge and limitation in the material itself, in the grain and density of the wood or the stone. Special tools are necessary for carving in stone or wood, in ivory, in plaster, or metal.

Clay, wax, and plasticine are most frequently used for modeling. When objects made of clay are allowed to dry and then are fired in a kiln they become *terra cotta* (literally, cooked earth). Sculpture made in clay, wax, or plasticine can be cast in plaster. The piece is surrounded by a plaster of Paris mold which is made in several parts. The mold is removed from the sculpture and set up in such a way that freshly mixed liquid plaster can be poured into it. (The inside of the mold has to be coated with oil or soap.) When the plaster is set, the mold is broken away. The piece of sculpture that emerges may then be modified by carving, tooling, and coloring if the sculptor so decides. The finished piece is called a plaster cast.

Sculpture in plaster or wax can also be cast in bronze or other metals by one or two methods: the sand-casting method and the "lost-wax" or *cire-perdue* method. The ancient bronzes of China (the owl "tsun" on page 82) and the great "Dancing Shiva," 43⅞" high (on page 43), from India were made by the lost-wax process, which is still being used today, both here and abroad. The original sculpture is made in wax and encased in a mold that has funnels and vents. The wax is heated and runs out. Hot liquid metal is poured in to fill up the spaces down to the last cracks and crevices. The mold is broken away after the metal has cooled, and the sculpture emerges. Sometimes, especially for very large pieces, a central core is used so that the final casting is hollow rather than solid.

Up to this point we have been speaking of free-standing sculpture, sculpture in the round. We should also make note of reliefs in which forms seem to emerge from a flat slab, a slab that can appropriately be set into a wall. Some reliefs have considerable projection: these are called high reliefs. Other are in low or "bas" relief. The processional frieze of the Parthenon is a notable example of relief carving.

To the methods of carving and modeling should be added a third approach, that of constructing a work directly by assembling parts that may

98

1. Japanese, ca. ninth century   NIKKO, THE SUN BODHISATTVA
2. Cambodian, tenth century   HEAD OF SHIVA
3. *Auguste Rodin*   BUST OF MADAME RODIN
4. *Edgar Degas*   DANCER LOOKING AT THE SOLE OF HER RIGHT FOOT
5. *Theodore Roszak*   MANDRAKE
6. Japanese, third–sixth century   HANIWA FIGURE

1. Wood (carved from one piece of Japanese yew)

2. Sandstone

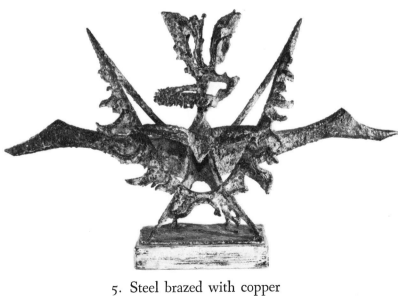

3. Bronze

SCULPTURE
MATERIALS AND
TECHNIQUES

4. Bronze

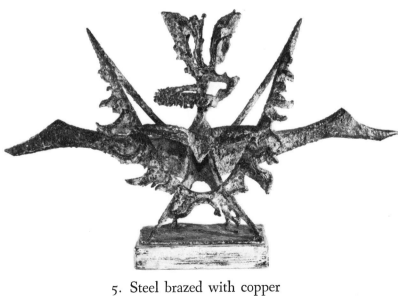

5. Steel brazed with copper

6. Terra cotta

be of different materials or may even include found objects. Paper, wood, glass, or cloth objects may be fastened together with glue, nails, screws, or even string and wire. When metal parts are used to create an assemblage they are usually welded together. Welded metal and laminated woods are characteristic of much contemporary sculpture. In the 1930's, Alexander Calder began making sculpture in which sheet-metal shapes, rods and wires, carefully balanced, move through space in a varying series of relationships. Sometimes a current of air, sometimes mechanical means set the forms in motion. Sculptures of this kind are known as "mobiles."

OTHER ARTS

In certain periods—such as the Gothic period in Europe, the seventeenth century in China and Japan, the eighteenth century in France—the so-called minor arts have been considered as important as the fine arts.

Alexander Calder
WHITE LOOPS AND RED
SPIRAL ON BLACK
Stabile-mobile, painted
steel and aluminum

Since bowls and pots define and enclose space, the art of the potter bears some relation to sculpture. Pots may be built by hand out of coils of clay, they may be turned on a potter's wheel, they may be poured in molds or built up of slabs. In the long history of ceramics, the most beautiful pots have been built up by hand or have been shaped by the hands that control the clay body as it is turned on the wheel. The color and character of glazes involves the same combination of art and chemistry as the making of glass.

The arts of stained glass, of the goldsmith and silversmith, of enameling, of cabinetmaking, of weaving, and of embroidery are beyond the scope of this discussion, but each one can open up a fascinating field of study. The arts as a whole seem always to flourish best whenever there is a lively interchange and understanding among architects, painters, and sculptors.

Materials and techniques of architecture range from construction of the simplest shelter to the technology of our modern cities. And since buildings exist in relation to other buildings and to their setting, architects concern themselves not only with individual structures but with the spaces between them. Thus it may be useful to design squares, parks, and neighborhoods, whole areas of our cities and of the countryside. Such large-scale design requires the co-operative effort of architects, engineers, landscape architects, planners, and many kinds of skilled technicians, along with the intelligent co-operation of alert and sensitive citizens.

CONSTITUTION PLAZA, HARTFORD, CONNECTICUT

9

The Traveler at Home and Abroad

When the French painter Eugène Delacroix made a journey to North Africa in 1832, he kept notebooks from which the page illustrated has been taken. This combination of pen and watercolor sketches and written notes reminded the artist of the colorful costumes, the fighting horses, the enclosed gardens, of all the sights and experiences that impressed him so deeply. For the next thirty years, Delacroix returned to these themes from time to time as you can see in such a celebrated painting as the "Algerian Women in Their Quarters" of 1834. The notes are almost as visual as the drawings:

Tangier, January 26.
With the *pasha*. The entrance to the castle: The guardsmen in the court, the façade, the lane between two walls. At the end, under a sort of vault, men seated, making a brown silhouette against a bit of sky.

The handsome man with the green sleeves.

The mulatto slave who poured the tea, yellow caftan and burnous attached in back, turban. The old man who gave the rose with *haik* and dark blue caftan.

The pasha with his two haiks or hoods, and the burnous beside. All three of them on a white mattress with a long square cushion covered with printed calico. A long narrow cushion of checkered cloth, another in horsehair, of various patterns; tips of the feet visible, the inkwell made of horn, various small objects lying about.

January 29.
Enchanting view while descending the length of the ramparts; after that the sea. Cactus and enormous aloes. Bamboo enclosure; patches of brown grass on the sand.

When returning, the contrast between the yellow and dry bamboo with the verdure of the rest. The mountains more nearly a brown green, dotted with blackish dwarfed shrubs. Huts.

The scene of the fighting horses. From the start, they stood up and fought with a fierceness which made me tremble for those gentlemen, but it was really admirable for a painting. I witnessed, I am certain, the most fantastic and graceful movements that Gros and Rubens could have imagined. . . .

On our return, superb landscapes to the right, the mountains of Spain in the tenderest tones, the sea a dark greenish blue like a fig, the hedges yellow at the top because of the bamboo, green at the base on account of the aloes.[1]

In our century, Paul Klee made a somewhat similar journey to North Africa. The year was 1914. The little watercolor sketch "Before the Gates of Kairouan" was presumably painted on the spot. Perhaps it is actually one of the sketches he mentions:

Thursday, 4.16. In the morning, painted outside the city; a gently diffused light falls, at once mild and clear. . . . An evening of colors as tender as they were clear. . . . Color possesses me. I don't have to pursue it. It will possess me always, I know it. That is the meaning of this happy hour: Color and I are one. I am a painter.

Friday, 4.17. In the morning, again painted outside the town, close to the wall, on a sand hill. Then went on a walk alone because I was so overflowing, out through a gate, where a few trees stand, rarities and rarity. When I got closer I determined it was a small park. A water basin filled with water plants, frogs, and tortoises.

Back through the dusty gardens before the town, painted a last watercolor while standing.[2]

Eighteen years later, Paul Klee made the painting called "Arab Song," which is much larger than the little watercolor. The memories of North Africa had gone down deep inside him and been transposed into this evocative, dreamlike image.

Some artists and writers find stimulus and refreshment in journeys to foreign places. For the Dutchman Van Gogh, brought up under the gray skies of the long northern European winter, the radiant light of Provence came as a revelation that challenged all his forces, all his talent. Other artists find wonder enough in the familiar world around them. Renoir once remarked that he could not understand why Gauguin went all the way to the South Seas when one could paint so well in Batignolles, in the suburbs of Paris.

In our own country, perhaps the writer most famous for his journal traveled only a few miles westward from his home in Concord, Massachusetts, to find a world in Walden Pond. What Thoreau saw there with the eyes of a naturalist and a poet he set down in such an original and personal way that his book *Walden* has become a kind of touchstone, a classic of American literature. Here is Thoreau, writing in his journal, on the subject of observation, or rather about those who do *not* observe the tiny green lichens that grow on the trunks of trees.

November 8, 1858

It is remarkable how little any but a lichenist will observe on the bark of trees. The mass of men have but the vaguest and most indefinite notion of mosses, as a sort of shreds, and fringes, and the world in which the lichenist dwells is much further from theirs than one side of this earth from the other. They see bark as if they saw it not.[3]

These pages from Delacroix and Klee, the quotation from Thoreau, are meant to call attention to the usefulness of keeping notebooks and sketchbooks, however modest, in order to sharpen observation, to strengthen memory, and to practice a shorthand skill in setting down verbal or pictorial impressions.

Notes may serve both as reminders of the past and as points of departure for the future. The following very personal and individual notes by the American painter Wolf Kahn were printed on the announcement of a one-man show in New York:

IN CONJUNCTION WITH THESE PICTURES:

Words: privacy, containedness, softness vs. sharpness, selectivity, rightness, contemplation, silence.

Things to do: go for a walk on a hazy day, gather mushrooms in wet woods, look out of window on foggy mornings, rake leaves in Fall, take ferry to Staten Island in winter.

Painters to like: Corot, Ryder, Giacometti, Morandi, Claude Lorrain, Marquet, Bonnard, Lester Johnson, Reinhardt, Jan Mueller.

Poets to like: Emily Dickinson, Rilke.

Things to ignore: the fads of the moment.

GREEK VASE PAINTING (detail)

Georges Braque HERAKLES

Georges Braque MUSICAL FORMS

Ambrosius Bosschaert the Elder STILL LIFE

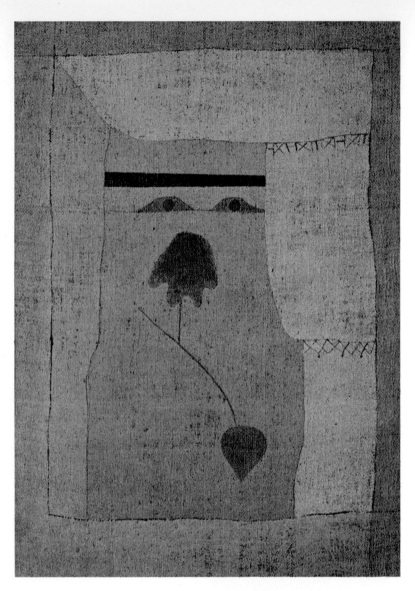

Paul Klee ARAB SONG

Paul Klee BEFORE THE GATES OF KAIROUAN

FRESCO

Giotto JOACHIM'S DREAM

TEMPERA

Fra Angelico THE CORONATION OF THE VIRGIN (detail)

OIL

Diego Velázquez   THE INFANTA MARGARITA IN A BLUE GOWN (detail)

PASTEL

Edgar Degas   RACEHORSES

Eugène Delacroix NOTEBOOK PAGE

Eugène Delacroix ALGERIAN WOMEN IN THEIR QUARTERS and (below) detail

Pablo Picasso THREE MUSICIANS

FUNERAL PROCESSION, Painting on Tomb (panel)

In an old sketchbook, I came across some words that I once jotted down about a flight over the coastline of New England. These simple notes brought back vividly the special quality of that bright summer afternoon.

Near Boston Airport: junkyard, like a mosaic
Low tide—wings over sea gulls
over Nahant
over Marblehead—racing—
Toy boats on a model glass sea
The Ipswich dunes
Dark shapes of the sea bottom
The blue immensity
Wake of a power boat
Whipped-cream clouds four stories high.

As the plane turned inland toward Bangor, I could see through a window across the aisle the shape of Mt. Katahdin standing up clearly to the northwest, and to the eastward the whole of Penobscot Bay, Isleboro, North Haven, Blue Hill, Deer Isle, Isle au Haut, and Mt. Desert, a tilting map.

For many of us nowadays, the telephone takes the place of letters, and a sequence of color slides becomes the modern substitute for the sketchbooks and diaries of Delacroix's time, or of an earlier day. If you are going to show slides even just to your own family and friends, remember that pictures will be more effective if they are sorted, weeded, and arranged with loving care. A long procession of views in which foreground, middle distance, and background are more or less uniformly seen becomes very monotonous. Vary the general views, landscapes, or cityscapes with close-ups, with significant details. A change of mood or a change of pace will help to keep your audience awake. Repetition can be deadly; choose your best slides and then cut the number you are going to show by half. And even if you go to the moon and bring back slides that are literally out of this world, fifty minutes will usually be long enough for the patience of your viewers.

There is another kind of journey that we can take without tickets or transportation, the dream journeys to which we are often inattentive. If you think you do not dream, keep a pad and pencil beside your bed for a few days. Before you are even half awake try to set down a few notes that will recall and record images that passed through your sleeping consciousness.

You may be surprised to discover the variety and individuality of your own dream images and you may gain a new understanding of certain kinds of fantasy and exaggeration in the world of art.

We have spoken about observation in the world of nature and about the heightened observation of travelers. Let us think briefly now about some of the ways in which we look at cities. A night flight over a great urban area can have the quality of a dream, a fairyland of lights in pinpoints, clusters, and chains. But the long ride in from an airport is likely to seem more like a nightmare confused with streaming traffic, shopping centers, and used-car lots.

How do we see a city when we approach it on an expressway—everything going past us at fifty or sixty miles an hour, and the cluster of tall buildings looming gradually larger as we approach? When we walk about, what shapes of open space, of steep canyons, of quiet corners attract our attention? Gertrude Stein once said about Los Angeles, "There isn't any there, there." Try to decide whether the city you know best has any *there*, any unique and characteristic areas.

The New England "green" may provide such a focus. The New Haven green where three churches stand in a row amid the surviving elms is, incidentally, one of the earliest examples of city planning in this country. And no traveler can return from Venice without a sense of the Piazza San Marco as an outdoor living room for all the people of Venice and their guests, complete with chairs, clock, views, and music, both sacred and secular.

Do you ever think about a building as being not only a functional shelter but also a work of imagination? Any building that gives a lift to the spirit begins in the mind of an architect, and yet how few of us can name the architects of buildings we know and admire. By their exterior masses, a building or a group of buildings may suggest strength or energy, rivalry or repose, aspiration or delight. Interior spaces by their form and scale, their light and color, make their own impression. The next time you are in a church or concert hall, a theater or auditorium, consider the shape of that interior space and what kind of impression you receive.

Finally, here are a few suggestions about visiting museums. If you are interested in drawing or design, remember that the exhibits in a natural history museum or the living animals at a zoo may be as fascinating to artists as to scientists. In any of our larger art museums it is important not to try to see too much at one time; whenever possible go at the least crowded times of day. In the big museums try to find a group of objects or paintings that have special appeal for you. Make notes or sketches, jot down questions to look up in a library, study and compare, make yourself familiar with this particular area, discover your favorites and then proceed to enlarge your horizons. Respect the works of art. Do not leave fingermarks anywhere, and make sure no careless pencil of yours ever leaves its trace on a unique and irreplaceable work of art that has been entrusted to a museum for preservation and care.

Those of you who are interested in becoming artists should remember the little story about Edouard Vuillard. When someone asked him how he came to be a painter, he replied, "I can say with Degas, 'my parents took us to the Louvre on Sunday afternoons. My brother slid on the polished floors and I looked at the pictures.'"

If you can establish a pattern or plan for visiting museums in this country, then when you travel abroad you will go about your sightseeing with more confidence than many of your fellow tourists. Most people try to see too much in too short a time.

Canaletto (Giovanni Antonio Canale) VIEW OF THE PIAZZA SAN MARCO

Gertrude Stein made a remark that makes more sense than one might at first think. She said, "I like museums, I like to look out of their windows." After an hour or so of intensive looking, suddenly when you come to a window you may see clouds, trees, or lawns through the eyes of Dutch landscape painters or French Impressionists or Chinese ink painters. You are seeing nature transformed by the imagination, or nature imitating art, or simply nature with heightened perception. This kind of experience is one of the by-products, not the main reward, of paintings. Fortunately we have the opportunity of seeing through the eyes of many artists and so eventually we may come to our own way of seeing.

(Left) *Henri Matisse* IN THE GARDENS OF THE ALHAMBRA (Right) A photograph of the gardens of the Cleveland Museum of Art as seen through a window. This is the view one comes upon immediately after the Matisse painting. Photograph by the author.

IO

The Immense Design

The opening paragraphs of this book pointed out that its purpose was twofold: to suggest ways of sharpening visual awareness when looking at works of art, especially paintings, and to consider some of the ways in which we look back and forth from the world of nature to the world of art. The painted or sculptured representations of animals and birds, and the development of landscape painting are the most obvious ways by which nature is translated into art. Columns of Egyptian temples suggest the growth of papyrus and lotus. In a formal statement carved in stone, stems become columns, buds or blossoms become capitals. Think of Chinese porcelains, with their cool elegance, in which the marvelously controlled crackle of the glaze recealls the veining of rocks or the shattering of ice. The elements of which the bowl is made, and the glaze itself, are part of the earth, shaped by human fingers and transformed by the fire of the kiln.

Even the language in which a Chinese writer describes brushstrokes in that apparently abstract art, the writing of Chinese characters, would be incomprehensible without a vivid experience of nature. You will notice that all his comparisons imply movement:

WINE CUP

> Like floating clouds across a clear sky;
> Like the twining branches of hanging wisteria;
> Like worms eating leaves;
> Like snakes fighting;
> Like fish swimming in water;
> Like a hawk after a bird;
> Like a galloping horse.

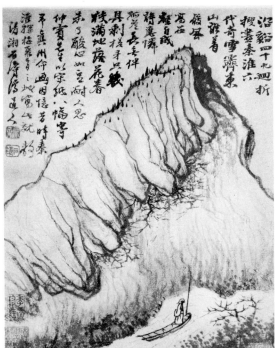

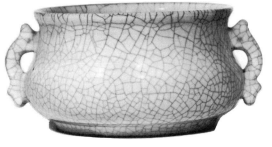

INCENSE BURNER

Shih-t'ao REMINISCENSES OF CH'IN HUAI RIVER

A celebrated Chinese painter of the eleventh century once said to his son, "Landscape is a big thing and should be viewed from a distance in order to grasp the scheme of hill and stream." In the tiny human figures on mountain paths, no more important than rocks, trees, and waterfalls, we sense the harmony of man and nature as it was expressed by the great artists of the Sung Dynasty.

In this country, when artists began to look at the new world around them, they could not see it in any way except through the conventions of European landscape painting, so strongly did habit influence their ways of seeing. They literally did not know what to make of the wilderness and so began, quite naturally, with the more settled areas. We seldom give enough credit to our own artists of the early nineteenth century who found a way to express "the scheme of hill and stream" here on a new continent—Asher Durand, Thomas Cole, and others of the Hudson River School, and later men like Frederick E. Church who went farther west.

Winslow Homer EARLY MORNING AFTER A STORM AT SEA

This challenge of painting in a new land, under a light different from the skies of Europe, was taken up by Winslow Homer, who lived from 1836 to 1910. Homer thought of himself as looking quite objectively at nature, and he usually painted in the bright light of day. At the same time that Homer was painting in the Adirondack Mountains, in the Caribbean, or on the coast of Maine, Alfred P. Ryder in a dingy studio in New York was painting his haunting, moonlit landscapes of an imagined world.

This brings us to a final question: Is the world of nature everything from the "pattern of fern and feather" to the immense design of a continent, or is it also the world within, nature transformed by the imagination?

Paul Klee knew that there was more to "reality" than the record or memory of what the eyes have seen.

A sailor of antiquity in his boat, enjoying himself and appreciating the comfortable accommodations. Ancient art represents the subject accordingly. And now: the experiences of a modern man, walking across deck of a steamer: 1. His own movement, 2. The movement of the ship which could be in the opposite direction, 3. The direction and the speed of the current, 4. The rotation of the earth, 5. Its orbit, and 6. The orbits of the stars and satellites around it.[1]

119

This fusion of the outer and the inner world that Klee describes is the concern of many poets and painters today. And we cannot say that this expression of an outer and an inner vision was not also of absorbing interest to Rembrandt, to El Greco, and to many other artists.

It is also true that artists today are preoccupied not so much with the continuity of man and nature as with its opposite, the alienation of man from nature and of man from man. That anxiety, tension, and rage can produce fine paintings is proved by Picasso's "Guernica," which expresses his anguished concern for the tragedy of the civil war in Spain. On the other hand, there are painters today who try to keep all emotion, all feeling out of their work. They want their paintings to have a purely visual impact; perhaps they are trying to tell us something about all the simultaneous sounds and images that come to us in this electronic age.

This book has tried to point out that there are many ways of seeing to explore. Look once more at the medieval "Spanish Funeral Procession" and at the twentieth-century Spanish painting "Three Musicians" by Picasso (on page 112). Try to think what these paintings, so separated in time, have in common, and how they differ; by what language of forms the artists are able to compel our attention, and what reverberations their paintings set in motion.

Perhaps the poet Rilke was right when he said that with nothing can one touch a work of art so little as with words. But a day may come when you will feel that you can apprehend the meaning of a work of art directly without the intervention of words, when you can put down the books and respond directly to the visual images before you.

> All architecture is what you do to it when you look upon it,
> (Did you think it was in the white or gray stone? or the lines of
> the arches and cornices?)
> All music is what awakes from you when you are reminded by
> the instruments,
> It is not the violins and the cornets . . . nor the score
> of the baritone singer . . .
> It is nearer and farther than they.
> —*Walt Whitman*

Notes

Page 5   T. S. Eliot, "Ash Wednesday," *The Complete Poems and Plays, 1909–1950* (New York: Harcourt, Brace & World, Inc.), 1952.

CHAPTER 1

Page 15   1. *John Marin, by Himself,* 1928, quoted in Dorothy Norman, ed., *The Selected Writings of John Marin* (New York: Pellegrini and Cudahy, 1949), p. 127. Reprinted with permission of John Marin, Jr.

CHAPTER 2

Page 19   1. W. H. Auden, ed., *Van Gogh, A Self-Portrait* (Greenwich, Connecticut: New York Graphic Society, 1961), p. 334. Used by permission of New York Graphic Society Ltd., Greenwich, Connecticut.

CHAPTER 3

Page 20   1. W. H. Auden, ed., *Van Gogh, A Self-Portrait,* p. 365.

CHAPTER 5

Page 46   1. W. H. Auden, ed., *Van Gogh, A Self-Portrait,* p. 320.

Page 48   2. Dag Hammarskjöld, *Markings,* Leif Sjöberg and W. H. Auden, trans. (New York: Alfred A. Knopf, Inc., 1964), p. 114. Reprinted by permission of Alfred A. Knopf, Inc. Copyright, © 1964 by Alfred A. Knopf, Inc. and Faber & Faber, Ltd.

INTERLUDE

Page 50   Edith Sitwell, *The Collected Poems* (New York: Vanguard Press, 1954), p. xx.

Page 52   William Butler Yeats, *The Collected Poems* (New York: The Macmillan Co., 1956), p. 292. Reprinted with permission of The Macmillan Company. Copyright 1940 Georgie Yeats.

Page 54   Arthur Waley, ed., *Translations From the Chinese* (New York: Alfred A. Knopf, Inc., 1919, 1941), p. 324. Copyright, 1919 by Alfred A. Knopf, Inc. Renewed, 1947 by Arthur Waley. Reprinted with permission of the publisher.

Page 55   Wallace Stevens, *The Collected Poems* (New York: Alfred A. Knopf, Inc., 1961), p. 165. Copyright, 1935, 1936, 1937, by Wallace Stevens. Renewed, 1964 by Holly Stevens Stephenson. Reprinted by permission of Alfred A. Knopf, Inc.

Page 56   Robert Frost, *The Complete Poems of Robert Frost* (New York: Henry Holt, 1949), p. 275. Copyright 1923 by Holt, Rinehart and Winston, Inc. Copyright 1951 by Robert Frost. Reprinted by permission of Holt, Rinehart and Winston, Inc.

Page 58   William Carlos Williams, *Pictures From Brueghel and Other Poems* (New York: New Directions, 1962), p. 5. Copyright © 1949, 1962 by William Carlos Williams. Reprinted by permission of the publisher.

Page 60   Justin O'Brien, ed. and trans., *The Maxims of Marcel Proust* (New York: Columbia University Press, 1948), p. 177.

Page 64   Marcel Proust, quoted in François Fosca, trans. by Gilbert Stuart, *The Eighteenth Century, Watteau to Tiepolo* (Geneva: Skira, 1952), p. 58.

Page 64   Albert Camus, *Discours de Suède* (Paris: Gallimard, 1958), p. 55. Reprinted by permission of Editions Gallimard and Alfred A. Knopf, Inc.

Pages
68–69   William Butler Yeats, *The Collected Poems*, p. 191. Reprinted with permission of The Macmillan Company from *The Tower* by William Butler Yeats. Copyright 1928 The Macmillan Company, renewed 1956 by Georgie Yeats.

Page 72   Lin Yutang, ed., *The Wisdom of China and India* (New York: Random House, 1942), p. 900.

CHAPTER 6
Page 75   1. Quoted in Alfred H. Barr, Jr., *Matisse—His Art and His Public* (New York: Museum of Modern Art, 1951), p. 119. Copyright 1951 by The Museum of Modern Art, and reprinted with its permission. "Notes d'un peintre" was originally published in *La Grande Revue*, Paris, December 23, 1908. The first complete English translation by Margaret Scolari Barr was published in *Henri Matisse,* The Museum of Modern Art, New York, 1931, and then again in *Matisse: His Art and His Public.*

CHAPTER 7
Page 87   1. Winston Churchill, *Painting as a Pastime* (New York: Whittlesey House, McGraw-Hill, 1950), pp. 13, 15.

CHAPTER 9
Pages
102–103 1. Walter Pach, trans., *The Journal of Eugène Delacroix* (New York: Crown Publishers, Inc., 1948), pp. 101, 102. Copyright © 1948, 1965 by Crown Publishers, Inc., and used by their permission.

Page 103   2. Felix Klee, ed., *The Diaries of Paul Klee, 1898–1918* (Berkeley and Los Angeles: University of California Press, 1964), pp. 297, 298.

Page 104   3. Bradford Torrey and Francis H. Allen, eds., *The Journal of Henry D. Thoreau* (Boston: Houghton Mifflin Co., 1949), Vol. XI, p. 296.

CHAPTER 10
Page 119   1. *The Inward Vision: Watercolors, Drawings, Writings by Paul Klee* (New York: Harry N. Abrams, Inc., 1958), from "Creative Credo," unpaged.

Books for Further Reading

WRITINGS OF ARTISTS

Auden, W. H., ed. *Van Gogh, A Self-Portrait*. Greenwich, Conn.: New York Graphic Society, 1961.

Cellini, Benvenuto, *Autobiography of Benevenuto Cellini*. Garden City, New York: Doubleday & Co., Inc. (Dolphin Books), 1961.

Delacroix, Eugène. *The Journal of Eugène Delacroix*. Translated and edited by Walter Pach. New York: Crown Publishers, Inc., 1948.

Goldwater, R., and Treves, Marco, eds. and trans. *Artists on Art, From the XIV to the XX Century*. New York: Pantheon Books, Inc., 1945.

Holt, Elizabeth Gilmore, ed. *A Documentary History of Art*. 2 vols. Garden City, New York: Doubleday & Co., Inc. (Anchor Books), 1957; *From the Classicists to the Impressionists*, vol. 3, 1966.

Kandinsky, Wasilly. *Concerning the Spiritual in Art*. New York: Wittenborn, Schultz, 1955.

Klee, Paul. *The Diaries of Paul Klee*. Edited by Felix Klee. Berkeley and Los Angeles: University of California Press, 1964.

Kuo Hsi. *An Essay on Landscape Painting*. Translated by S. Sakanishi. Wisdom of the East series. London: Murray, 1935.

Leonardo da Vinci. *The Notebooks: A New Selection*. Selected by Pamela Taylor. New York: New American Library (Mentor Books), 1960.

Marin, John. *Letters of John Marin*. Edited with an Introduction by Herbert J. Seligmann. New York: Privately printed, 1931.

Shahn, Ben. *The Shape of Content*. New York: Random House, Inc. (Vintage Books), 1957.

ESSAYS AND CRITICISM

Arnheim, Rudolf. *Art and Visual Perception, A Psychology of the Creative Eye*. Berkeley and Los Angeles: University of California Press, 1954.

Clark, Sir Kenneth. *Looking at Pictures*. New York: Holt, Rinehart & Winston, Inc., 1960.

———. *The Nude: A Study in Ideal Form*. New York: Pantheon Books, Inc., 1953. (Also available in a paperback Doubleday Anchor Book edition.)

Elsen, Albert E. *Purposes of Art*. New York: Holt, Rinehart & Winston, Inc., 1962.

Fleming, William. *Arts and Ideas,* third edition. New York: Holt, Rinehart & Winston, Inc., 1968. (Useful for the relations between painting, architecture, sculpture, and music.)

Kepes, Gyorgy. *Language of Vision.* Chicago: Paul Theobald and Co., 1945.

———. *The New Landscape in Art and Science.* Chicago: Paul Theobald and Co., 1955.

Malraux, André. *Museum Without Walls.* Translated by Stuart Gilbert and Francis Price. Garden City, New York: Doubleday & Co., Inc. (paperback), 1967.

Warner, Langdon. *The Enduring Art of Japan.* London: Evergreen Books, 1958.

Zucker, Paul. *Styles in Painting.* New York: Dover Publications, 1963.

HISTORY OF ART

Akiyama, Terukazu. *Japanese Painting.* Translated by James Emmons. Geneva: Skira, 1961.

Cahill, James. *Chinese Painting.* Geneva: Skira, 1960.

Craven, Thomas. *The Rainbow Book of Art.* Cleveland and New York: The World Publishing Company, 1956. (Written for young people.)

Gombrich, Ernst H. *The Story of Art,* revised edition. New York: Phaidon Press, 1966.

Friedlaender, Walter F. *From David to Delacroix.* Cambridge, Massachusetts: Harvard University Press, 1952.

Haftmann, Werner. *Painting in the Twentieth Century.* 2 vols. New York: Frederick A. Praeger, Inc., 1961.

Janson, H. W. *History of Art.* New York: Harry N. Abrams, Inc., 1963.

Larkin, Oliver. *Art and Life in America.* New York: Henry Holt, 1949.

Lee, Sherman E. *A History of Far Eastern Art.* Englewood Cliffs, New Jersey: Prentice-Hall, Inc.; New York: Harry N. Abrams, Inc., 1964.

Leymarie, Jean. *Impressionism.* Translated by James Emmons. 2 vols. Geneva: Skira, 1955.

Munro, Eleanor C. *The Golden Encyclopedia of Art: Painting, Sculpture, Architecture, and Ornament, From Prehistoric Times to the Twentieth Century,* revised edition. New York: Golden Press, 1964.

The Praeger Picture Encyclopedia of Art. New York: Frederick A. Praeger, Inc., 1958.

Raynal, Maurice. *The Nineteenth Century: New Sources of Emotion from Goya to Gauguin.* Translated by James Emmons. Geneva: Skira, 1951.

Rewald, John. *History of Impressionism.* Revised and enlarged edition. New York: Museum of Modern Art, 1961.

Richardson, E. P. *A Short History of Painting in America.* New York: Thomas Y. Crowell Co., 1963.

MYTHOLOGY AND RELIGION

Appleton, Le Roy H., and Bridges, Stephen. *Symbolism in Liturgical Art.* New York: Charles Scribner's Sons, 1959.

Attwater, Donald, ed. *The Penguin Dictionary of Saints.* Baltimore: Penguin Books, Inc., 1965.

Bulfinch, Thomas. *Bulfinch's Mythology.* New York: Thomas Y. Crowell Co., 1947.

Coomaraswamy, Ananda K. *The Dance of Shiva*. New York: Noonday Press, Farrar, Straus & Co., 1957.

Ferguson, G. *Signs and Symbols in Christian Art*. New York: Oxford University Press, (Hesperides Books), 1961.

Hamilton, Edith. *Mythology*. Boston: Little, Brown & Company, 1942. (Also available in a paperback New American Library edition).

Harrison, G. B., ed. *The Bible for Students of Literature and Art*. Garden City, New York: Doubleday & Co., Inc. (Anchor Books), 1964.

Scherer, Margaret. *Legends of Troy*. New York: Phaidon Press, 1963.

Smith, Huston. *The Religions of Man*. New York: Harper & Row (Perennial Library), 1958.

Yohannan, John D., ed. *A Treasury of Asian Literature*. New York: John Day Co., 1956. (Also available in a paperback New American Library Mentor edition).

PAINTING: INDIVIDUAL ARTISTS

A series called *The Taste of Our Time,* published by Skira and distributed by The World Publishing Company, includes biographical and critical studies of many painters. Among those discussed in this book are:

Degas	Manet
Delacroix	Monet
Dürer	Picasso
Van Gogh	Rembrandt
El Greco	Renoir
Ingres	Titian
Klee	Turner

Goodrich, Lloyd. *Winslow Homer*. New York: The Macmillan Co., 1944.

Grohmann, Will. *Paul Klee*. New York: Harry N. Abrams, Inc., 1956.

Liberman, Alexander. *Artist in His Studio*. New York: The Viking Press (Studio Books), 1960.

Rosenberg, Jakob. *Rembrandt*. 2 vols. Cambridge, Massachusetts: Harvard University Press, 1948.

Schapiro, Meyer. *Paul Cézanne*. New York: Harry N. Abrams, Inc., 1952.

————. *Vincent van Gogh*. New York: Harry N. Abrams, Inc., 1950.

Seitz, William C. *Monet*. New York: Harry N. Abrams, Inc., 1960.

Vasari, Giorgio. *The Lives of the Artists*. A selection translated by George Bull. Baltimore: Penguin Books, Inc., 1965.

PRINTS AND DRAWINGS

Hayter, S. W. *New Ways of Gravure,* second edition. New York: Oxford University Press, 1966.

Holme, Bryan. *Drawings To Live With*. New York: The Viking Press, 1966.

Ivins, William M., Jr. *How Prints Look*. New York: Metropolitan Museum of Art, 1943.

Nicolaïdes, Kimon. *The Natural Way To Draw*. Boston: Houghton Mifflin Co., 1941.

Rosenberg, Jakob. *Great Draughtsmen from Pisanello to Picasso*. Cambridge, Massachusetts: Harvard University Press, 1959.

Sachs, Paul J. *Modern Prints and Drawings.* New York: Alfred A. Knopf, Inc., 1954.
———. *The Pocket Book of Great Drawings.* New York: Washington Square Press, 1961.
Toney, Anthony. *150 Masterpieces of Drawing.* New York: Dover Publications, 1963.
Wechsler, Herman J. *Great Prints and Printmakers.* New York: Harry N. Abrams, Inc., 1967.

ARCHITECTURE

Andrews, Wayne. *Architecture, Ambition, and Americans: A Social History of American Architecture.* New York: The Free Press, 1964.
———. *Architecture in America: A Photographic History From the Colonial Period to the Present.* New York: Atheneum Publishers, 1960.
Hamlin, Talbot F. *Architecture Through the Ages,* revised edition. New York: G. P. Putnam's Sons, 1953.
Jacobs, Jane. *Death and Life of Great American Cities.* New York: Random House, Inc. (Vintage Books) 1961.
Mumford, Lewis. *Sticks and Stones.* New York: W. W. Norton & Co., 1933.
Nervi, Pier Luigi. *Aesthetics and Technology in Building.* Translated by Robert Einaudi. Cambridge, Massachusetts: Harvard University Press, 1965.
Neutra, Richard. *Survival Through Design.* New York: Oxford University Press, 1954.
Richards, J. M. *An Introduction to Modern Architecture,* Baltimore: Penguin Books, Inc., 1962.
Sullivan, Louis. *Kindergarten Chats and Other Writings.* New York: Wittenborn, Schultz, 1947.
Tunnard, Christopher. *The City of Man.* New York: Charles Scribner's Sons, 1953.
Wright, Frank Lloyd. *An Autobiography,* revised edition. New York: Duell, Sloan & Pearce, 1943.

SCULPTURE

Boardman, John. *Greek Art.* New York: Frederick A. Praeger, Inc. (paperback), 1964.
Giedion-Welcker, Carola. *Contemporary Sculpture and Evolution in Volume and Space,* third revised edition. New York: Wittenborn and Company, 1960.
Read, Sir Herbert. *The Art of Sculpture.* New York: Museum of Modern Art, 1952.
———. *A Concise History of Modern Sculpture.* New York: Frederick A. Praeger, Inc., 1964.
Sweeney, James J. *Alexander Calder.* New York: Museum of Modern Art, 1951.

PHOTOGRAPHY

Adams, Ansel. *These We Inherit: The Parklands of America.* San Francisco: The Sierra Club, 1962.

Feininger, Andreas. *The Anatomy of Nature*. New York: Crown Publishers, Inc., 1956.

Newhall, Nancy. *Ansel Adams Volume 1: The Eloquent Light*. San Francisco: The Sierra Club, 1963.

Pollack, Peter. *The Picture History of Photography*. New York: Harry N. Abrams, Inc., 1958.

Steichen, Edward J. *The Family of Man*. New York: Museum of Modern Art, 1955.

MATERIALS OF THE ARTIST

Cennini, Cennino. *The Craftsman's Handbook, "Il Libro dell'Arte."* Translated and edited by Daniel V. Thompson, Jr. New York: Dover Publications, 1954.

Constable, William G. *The Painter's Workshop*. New York: Oxford University Press, 1954.

Herberts, Kurt. *The Complete Book of Artists' Techniques*. New York: Frederick A. Praeger, Inc., 1958.

Mayer, Ralph. *Artist's Handbook of Materials and Techniques*. New York: The Viking Press, 1957.

Thompson, D. V. *The Materials and Techniques of Medieval Painting*. New York: Dover Publications, Inc., 1956.

Watrous, James. *The Craft of Old-Master Drawings*. Madison: University of Wisconsin Press, 1957.

COLLECTORS AND COLLECTING

Constable, William G. *Art Collecting in the United States of America: An Outline of a History*. London: Thomas Nelson & Sons, 1964.

Gimpel, René. *Diary of an Art Dealer*. Translated by John Rosenberg. New York: Farrar, Straus & Giroux, Inc., 1966.

Saarinen, Aline B. *The Proud Possessors: The Lives, Times, and Tastes of Some Adventurous American Art Collectors*. New York: Random House, Inc., 1958.

THE WORLD OF NATURE

Adams, Ansel, and Newhall, Nancy. *This Is the American Earth*. San Francisco: The Sierra Club, 1960.

Blossfeldt, Karl. *Art Forms in Nature*. New York: Weyhe, 1929.

Carson, Rachel. *The Sea Around Us*. New York: New American Library (Mentor Books), 1959.

———. *The Sense of Wonder*. New York: Harper & Row, 1965.

Cousteau, Jacques-Yves, and Dugan, James. *The Living Sea*. New York: Harper & Row, 1963.

———, and Dumas, Frédéric. *The Silent World*. New York: Harper & Bros., 1953.

Douglas, William O. *My Wilderness, East to Katahdin*. Garden City, New York: Doubleday & Co., Inc., 1961.

Eisley, Loren. *The Immense Journey*. New York: Random House, Inc. (Vintage Books), 1956.

Engel, Leonard, and the Editors of *Life*. *The Sea*. New York: Times, Inc. (Life Nature Library), 1961.

127

Farb, Peter, and the Editors of *Life*. *The Forest*. New York: Time, Inc. (Life Nature Library), 1961.

Feininger, Andreas. *Forms of Nature and Life*. New York: The Viking Press (Studio Books), 1966.

Krutch, Joseph Wood. *The Voice of the Desert, A Naturalist's Interpretation*. New York: William Sloane Associates, 1954.

Porter, Eliot. *In Wildness Is the Preservation of the World*. Selections from Henry David Thoreau and Photographs by Eliot Porter. San Francisco: The Sierra Club, 1962. (Also available in a paperback edition.)

Thoreau, Henry David. *Walden: Or, Life in the Woods*. With a Preface by Joseph Wood Krutch. New York: Libra Publishers, Inc., 1960.

Index

(Page numbers in italics refer to illustrations.)

Illustrations

ADAMS, Ansel. *Fern in Rain, Mount Rainier National Park.* Photograph. Sierra Club, San Francisco, **51**

ANGELICO, Fra (1387–1455). *The Coronation of the Virgin* (detail), ca. 1430–1440. Tempera on panel (82¾ x 83½"). Musée du Louvre, Paris, **108 below**

Arras Tapestry, Scene From a Novel, ca. 1420. Collections Musée des Arts Décoratifs, Paris, **67**

Athenian Bowl (detail), eighth–seventh century B.C. Chariots. Staatlichen Antikensammlungen, Munich, **105 above**

Baby in Red Chair, 1800–1825. Oil on canvas. Abby Aldrich Rockefeller Folk Art Collection, Williamsburg, Virginia, **54**

BOSSCHAERT THE ELDER, Ambrosius (ca. 1573–1645). *Still life.* Oil on copper (14 x 11½"). The Cleveland Museum of Art, Gift of Carrie Moss Halle in Memory of Salmon Portland Halle, **106**

BRANCUSI, Constantin (1876–1957). *Torso,* 1917. Brass (18⅜ x 12 x 6⅝"). The Cleveland Museum of Art, Hinman B. Hurlbut Collection, **29 left**

BRAQUE, Georges (1882–1963). *Herakles,* 1931. Incised plaster (73 x 41¼"). Collection Aimé Maeght, Paris; Authorization ADAGP 1968 by French Reproduction Rights, Inc., **105 left.** *Musical Forms,* Philadelphia Museum of Art, The Louise and Walter Arensberg Collection; Authorization ADAGP 1968 by French Reproduction Rights, Inc., **105 right**

A Bridal Pair, ca. 1470. German. Swabian School, Ulm. Tempera on fir panel (25½ x 15½"). The Cleveland Museum of Art, Delia E. and L. E. Holden Funds, **30 right**

BRUEGHEL, Pieter (ca. 1525–1569). *Hunters in the Snow,* 1565. Oil on canvas (46 x 63¾"). Kunsthistorisches Museum, Vienna, **59**

CALDER, Alexander (1898–   ). *White Loops and Red Spiral on Black*. Stabile-mobile, painted steel and aluminum (h: 30½″). The Cleveland Museum of Art, Gift of Halle Bros. Co., **100**

CANALE (called Canaletto), Giovanni Antonio (1697–1768). *View of the Piazza San Marco and the Piazzetta Towards San Giorgio Maggiore*. Oil on canvas (53 x 91½″). The Cleveland Museum of Art, Purchase, Leonard C. Hanna, Jr., Bequest, **115**

CEZANNE, Paul (1839–1906). *The Pigeon Tower at Montbriand*, 1894–1896. Oil on canvas (25¼ x 31½″). The Cleveland Museum of Art, **38 below**. *Still Life With Apples*, 1895–1900. Oil on canvas (27 x 36½″). Collection, The Museum of Modern Art, New York. Lillie P. Bliss Collection, **65**

CHAO MENG-FU (1254–1322). *Bamboo, Rocks, and Lonely Orchids* (detail), Chinese, Yüan Dynasty. Handscroll, ink on paper (19⅞ x 56¾″). The Cleveland Museum of Art, John L. Severance Fund, **25**

CHARDIN, Jean Simeon (1699–1779). *The Skate*, 1728. Oil on canvas (45 x 57½″). Musée du Louvre, Paris, **65 above**

CH'IEN HSUAN (1235–1290). *Early Autumn* (detail), Chinese, Yüan Dynasty. Handscroll, ink and color on paper (10½ x 47¼″). The Detroit Institute of Arts, **19**

CHURCH, Frederick Edwin (1826–1900). *Twilight in the Wilderness*. Oil on canvas (40 x 64″). The Cleveland Museum of Art, Mr. and Mrs. William H. Marlatt Fund, **118 below**

COLE, Thomas (1801–1848). *Schroon Mountains, The Adirondacks*. Oil on canvas (39⅜ x 63″). The Cleveland Museum of Art, Hinman B. Hurlbut Collection, **118 above**

DAUMIER, Honoré (1808–1879). *Connoisseurs*. Watercolor, charcoal, and pencil (10¼ x 7⅝″). The Cleveland Museum of Art, Dudley P. Allen Fund, **89 and detail, jacket**

DEGAS, Hilaire Germain Edgar (1834–1917). *Dancer Looking at the Sole of Her Right Foot*. Bronze (h: 18″). The Cleveland Museum of Art, Hinman B. Hurlbut Collection, **99**; *Racehorses*, ca. 1883–1885. Pastel (21¼ x 24¾″). The National Gallery of Canada, Ottawa, **109 below**

DE KOONING, Willem (1904–   ). *Figure*. Oil on cardboard (17⅞ x 14″). Contemporary Collection of The Cleveland Museum of Art, **46**

DELACROIX, Eugène (1798–1863). *Algerian Women in Their Quarters*, 1834. Oil on canvas (71 x 90″). Musée du Louvre, Paris, **111**. *Notebook Page*. Pen and watercolor (7½ x 5″). Musée du Louvre, Paris **110**. *St. George and the Dragon*, 1847. Oil on canvas (11 x 14″). Musée du Louvre, Paris, **33 below**.

Wild Horse, 1828. Lithograph (9 x 8⅞"). The Cleveland Museum of Art, a Twenty-fifth Anniversary Gift, Mr. and Mrs. Lewis B. Williams Collection, **95**

FAN K'UAN (early eleventh century). *Traveling Among Streams and Mountains.* Hanging Scroll. Ink and light color on silk (69 x 29¼"). Collection of the National Palace Museum, Taipei, Taiwan, Republic of China, **34**

FEININGER, Lyonel (1871–1956). *Houses in Old Paris.* Woodcut (12⁵⁄₁₆ x 9¹⁵⁄₁₆"). The Cleveland Museum of Art, Gift of the Print Club of Cleveland, **95**

FRAGONARD, Jean Honoré (1732–1806). *Scene in a Park.* Drawing, pen and wash (7⅝ x 9⅞"). The Cleveland Museum of Art, Dudley P. Allen Fund, **24**

Funeral Procession (late thirteenth century). Tomb of Sancho Saiz de Carillo (19¾ x 34¼"). Ayuntamiento de Barcelona, Museos de arte, Barcelona, **112 below**

GALLO, Frank (1933–   ). *Male Image.* Epoxy resin (no. 1 in an edition of 5) (63 x 20 x 31" on base 2 x 4 x 31"). Contemporary Collection of The Cleveland Museum of Art, **48**

GAUGUIN, Paul (1848–1903). *The House of the Maori,* 1891. Oil on canvas (28⅞ x 36"). Private Collection, **66**

GEOGHEGAN, John. *Boy Behind Staircase. Grand Piano.* Photographs. Courtesy of Western Reserve Academy, **85**

GEROME, Léon (1824–1904). *Pygmalion and Galatea.* Oil on canvas (35 x 27"). The Metropolitan Museum of Art, Gift of Louis C. Raegner, 1927, **45 left**

GIOTTO (ca. 1276–ca. 1337). *Joachim's Dream* (detail). Fresco in the Cappella degli Scrovegni. Courtesy of Museo Civico de Padua, Padua, **108 above**

GOGH, Vincent van (1853–1890). *Wheat Field With Cypresses,* 1889. Oil on canvas (28½ x 36"). Reproduced by courtesy of the Trustees, The National Gallery, London, **38 above**

Haniwa Figure. Japan, Kofun Period, 200–552. Terra cotta (23 x 12"). The Cleveland Museum of Art, James Parmelee Fund, **99**

Head of Shiva. Cambodia, tenth century. Stone (h: 16½"). The Cleveland Museum of Art, John L. Severance Fund, **99**

The Holy Martyrs. After 526. Fragment, Mosaic in the Nave. Soprintendenza ai Monumenti, Ravenna. Chiesa di S. Apollinare Nuovo, **69**

The Holy Virgins. After 526. Fragment, Mosaic in the Nave. Soprintendenza ai Monumenti, Ravenna. Chiesa di S. Apollinare Nuovo, **68**

HOMER, Winslow (1836–1910). *Early Morning After a Storm at Sea.* Oil on canvas (30¼ x 50"). The Cleveland Museum of Art, J. H. Wade Collection, **119**

INGLIS, John. *Pond at Dawn.* Photograph. Courtesy of Western Reserve Academy, **86**

INGRES, Jean Auguste Dominique (1780–1867). *Portrait of Madame Raoul-Rochette,* 1830. Drawing, pencil (12⅝ x 9½″). The Cleveland Museum of Art, Purchase from the J. H. Wade Fund, **91.** *Reclining Odalisque.* Oil on canvas (35 13/16 x 64 9/16″). Musée du Louvre, Paris, **33 above**

KIRCHNER, Ernst Ludwig (1880–1938). *Mountain Landscape With Fir Trees.* Drawing, pencil and brush and India ink (13 3/16 x 19⅞″). The Cleveland Museum of Art, Delia E. and L. E. Holden Funds, **91**

KLEE, Paul (1879–1940). *Arab Song,* 1932. Oil on canvas (36 x 24¼″). The Phillips Collection, Washington, D. C.; Authorization SPADEM 1968 by French Reproduction Rights, Inc., **107 above.** *Before the Gates of Kairouan,* 1914. Watercolor (8⅛ x 12⅜″). Paul Klee Stiftung, Kuntsmuseum Bern (Paul Klee Foundation, Museum of Fine Arts, Bern); Authorization SPADEM 1968 by French Reproduction Rights, Inc., **107 below**

LIANG K'AI (fl. mid-thirteenth century). *Li Po Chanting a Poem.* Hanging Scroll (cropped at top). Ink on paper (30⅞ x 12⅛″). Tokyo National Musuem, **72**

LICHTENSTEIN, Roy (1923–). *Portrait of Holly.* Oil on canvas (81 x 81″). Collection of Mr. and Mrs. Horace H. Solomon, **47 left**

Lu: Incense Burner. Chinese, Sung Dynasty, 960–1279. Kuan Ware, porcellaneous stoneware (diameter: 6⅛″). The Cleveland Museum of Art, Mr. and Mrs. Severance A. Millikin Collection, **17**

MANET, Edouard (1832–1883). *The Fifer,* 1886. Oil on canvas (62¾ x 38½″). Musée du Louvre, Paris, **39 above.** *Luncheon on the Grass* (Le dejeuner sur l'herbe), 1863. Oil on canvas (83⅛ x 106¼″). Musée du Louvre, Paris, **45 right**

MARIN, John (1870–1953). *Maine Islands.* Watercolor (16¾ x 20″). The Phillips Collection, Washington, D. C., **15**

MATISSE, Henri (1869–1954). *In the Gardens of the Alhambra.* Oil on canvas (18 x 14⅞″). The Cleveland Museum of Art, Leonard C. Hanna, Jr., Collection, **116 left**

McCULLOUGH, Joseph. *Broken Window Panes.* Photograph, **28**

MECKENEM, Israhel van (fifteenth century). *The Organ Player and His Wife.* Engraving (6 9/16 x 4⅜″). The Cleveland Museum of Art, Delia E. Holden Fund, **95**

MIECZKOWSKI, Edwin (1923–). *Waverly Place.* Acrylic on panel (23½ x 23½″). Collection of Mr. and Mrs. William D. Wixom, **47 right**

MODIGLIANI, Amedeo (1884–1920). *Portrait of a Girl.* Oil on canvas (25¾ x 19″). The Cleveland Museum of Art, Gift of Hanna Fund, **29**

MONDRIAN, Piet (1872–1944). *Painting No. 1,* 1921. Oil on canvas (38 x 24″). Wallraf-Richartz-Museum an der Rechtschule, Köln, **63**

MONET, Claude (1840–1926). *Antibes*. Oil on canvas (25¼ x 36"). The Cleveland Museum of Art, Gift of Mr. and Mrs. J. H. Wade, **39 below**

MOORE, Janet Gaylord. *From a Museum Window*. Photograph, **116**

MOTHERWELL, Robert (1915–   ). *Mallarmé's Swan*. Collage (43 x 35½"). Contemporary Collection of The Cleveland Museum of Art, **80**

Nikko, The Sun Bodhisattva. Japan, Konin Period, ca. 800. Carved from one block of Japanese yew (18¾"). The Cleveland Museum of Art, John L. Severance Fund, **99**

One of a Pair of Lions. Dahomey, Africa. Wood (23½ x 8½ x 14⅛"). The Cleveland Museum of Art, Gift of Mrs. Ralph M. Coe, in Memory of Ralph M. Coe, **128**

Phoenix Mutual Building and Constitution Plaza, Hartford, Connecticut. Howard Sochurek, *Life* Magazine © Time, Inc., All rights reserved, **101**

PICASSO, Pablo (1881–   ). *Girl Before a Mirror*, 1932. Oil on canvas (63¾ x 51¼"). Collection, The Museum of Modern Art, New York. Gift of Mrs. Simon Guggenheim; Authorization SPADEM 1968 by French Reproduction Rights, Inc., **71 and detail, jacket**. *The Old Guitarist*. Oil on canvas (48⅛ x 32⁷⁄₁₆"). The Art Institute of Chicago, Helen Birch Bartlett Memorial Collection; Authorization SPADEM 1968 by French Reproduction Rights, Inc., **55**. *Reclining Nude*, 1938. Drawing, pen and ink on paper (10¾ x 13⅞"). Contemporary Collection of The Cleveland Museum of Art, **91**. *Three Musicians*, 1921 summer. Oil on canvas (79 x 87¾"). Collection, The Museum of Modern Art, New York. Mrs. Simon Guggenheim Fund; Authorization SPADEM 1968 by French Reproduction Rights, Inc., **112 above**

PIRANESI, Giovanni Battista (1720–1778). *The Prisons: An Immense Interior With a Drawbridge*. Etching (21⁹⁄₁₆ x 16⅛"). The Cleveland Museum of Art, Dudley P. Allen Fund, **95**

REMBRANDT VAN RIJN (1606–1669). *The Artist in His Studio*, 1626–1628. Oil on canvas (10 x 12½"). The Zoe Oliver Sherman Collection. Given in Memory of Lillie Oliver Poor. Courtesy, Museum of Fine Arts, Boston, **60**. *Self-portrait*, 1659. Oil on canvas (33¼ x 26"). National Gallery of Art, Washington, D. C. Andrew Mellon Collection, **40 and detail, jacket**. *The Three Crosses*, 1653. Etching and drypoint (14¾ x 17⅜"). The Cleveland Museum of Art, Bequest of Ralph King and Purchase from the J. H. Wade Fund, **95**

RENOIR, Pierre Auguste (1841–1919). *The Luncheon of the Boating Party* (Le déjeuner des canotiers). Oil on canvas (51 x 68"). The Phillips Collection, Washington, D. C.; Authorization SPADEM 1968 by French Reproduction Rights, Inc., **17 and detail, jacket**

RODIN, Auguste (1840–1917). *Bust of Madame Rodin (Mignon)*. Bronze (h: 20"). The Cleveland Museum of Art, In Memory of Ralph King. Gift of Mrs. Ralph King, Ralph T. Woods, Charles G. King, and Frances King Schafer, **99**

ROSZAK, Theodore (1907–   ). *Mandrake*. Steel brazed with copper (25½ x 40 x 13¾"). The Cleveland Museum of Art, Gift of the Cleveland Society for Contemporary Art, **99**

ROTHKO, Mark (1903–   ). *Brown and Black on Plum*. Oil on canvas. Dr. Franz Meyer, Basel, **37**. *Red, White and Brown*, 1957. Oil on canvas (99½ x 81¾"). Kuntsmuseum, Basel, **detail, jacket**

RUBENS, Peter Paul (1557–1640). *Rubens With His First Wife, Isabella Brant* (ca. 1609). Oil on canvas attached to wood (52 x 68"). Alte Pinakotek, Bayerischen Staatsgemaldesammlungen, Munich, **30 left**

RYDER, Albert Pinkham (1847–1917). *The Race Track or Death on a Pale Horse*. Oil on canvas (28¼ x 35¼"). The Cleveland Museum of Art, Purchase, J. H. Wade Fund, **27**

SHAPARD, Jane Watt. *Chinese Bronze Owl*. Collage. Gray, black, and white paper with ink and crayon (24 x 18"), **82**

SHIH-T'AO (Tao-chi) (1641–ca. 1720). *Reminiscences of Ch'in Huai River* (Album of 8 leaves), Chinese, Ch'ing Dynasty. Ink and color on paper (10¹⁄₁₆ x 7¹⁵⁄₁₆"). The Cleveland Museum of Art, John L. Severance Fund, **117**. *Spring on the Min River*. Hanging Scroll. Ink and color on paper (15⅜ x 20⁷⁄₁₆"). The Cleveland Museum of Art, John L. Severance Fund, **88**

Shiva Nataraja, South Indian, eleventh century. Copper (43⅞ x 40"). The Cleveland Museum of Art, Purchase from the J. H. Wade Fund, **43**

SMELTZ, Barbara. *Assemblage in a Sardine Can*. Foil, wire, sequins, etc., **84**

SOTATSU (1576–1643). Japanese, Tokugawa Period. *Sano no Watari: Crossing at Sano*. Single screen, ink and slight color on paper (51 x 49⅛). The Cleveland Museum of Art, John L. Severance Fund, **72**

SOULAGES, Pierre (1919–   ). *Painting*, May 1953. Oil on canvas (76⅜ x 51¼"). The Solomon R. Guggenheim Museum, **18**

TIEPOLO, Giovanni Domenico (1727–1804). *The Spring Shower*. Pen and bistre ink and bistre wash (11⅝ x 16¼"). The Cleveland Museum of Art, Purchase from the J. H. Wade Fund, **91**

TITIAN (ca. 1488–1576). *The Entombment*, 1559. Oil on canvas (54 x 68¾"). The Prado, Madrid, **36**

TURNER, J. M. W. (1775–1851). *Rain, Steam, and Speed*. Oil on canvas (36 x 48"). Reproduced by courtesy of the Trustees, The National Gallery, London, **35**

Tsun: Owl. Chinese, Shang or Early Western Chou Period (1027–771 B.C.). Bronze (h: 8¼"). The Cleveland Museum of Art, John L. Severance Fund, **82**

UTAMARO, Kitagawa (1753–1806). *One of the Seven Women Seen in a Mirror* (Sugatami Shichi Nin Kesho), ca. 1790. Color wood-block print (10 x 11"). Private Collection, **70 and detail, jacket**

VELAZQUEZ, Diego (1599–1660). *The Infanta Margarita in a Blue Gown* (detail), ca. 1659. Oil on canvas (50 x 42⅛"). Kunsthistorisches Museum, Vienna, **109 above**

VERMEER, Jan (1632–1675). *The Artist in His Studio,* ca. 1665. Oil on canvas (47¼ x 39¼"). Kunsthistorisches Museum, Vienna, **61**

WATTEAU, Jean Antoine (1684–1721). *Study for the Romancer.* Drawing, red and black chalk (13¾ x 10⅝"). The Cleveland Museum of Art, Dudley P. Allen Fund, **91**

Wine Cup. Chinese, Ming Dynasty, Mark and Reign of Ch'eng Hua, 1465–1487. Porcelain with "three color" decoration (h: 1⅞"). The Cleveland Museum of Art, John L. Severance Fund, **117**

WU PIN (1573–1620). *Greeting the Spring* (detail), 1600. Chinese, Ming Dynasty. Handscroll, ink and color on paper (13¾ x 51¹¹⁄₁₆"). The Cleveland Museum of Art, John L. Severance Fund, **53**

WITTE, Emanuel de (ca. 1617–1692). *Interior With a Harpsichord,* ca. 1665–1670. Oil on canvas (30¼ x 40⅞"). Dutch State Collection on Loan to the Museum Boymansvan Beuningen, Rotterdam, copyright reserved, **62**

All other drawings are by Janet Gaylord Moore.

ABOUT THE AUTHOR

Janet Gaylord Moore, an Associate Curator at the Cleveland Museum of Art, is also a well-known painter and a former art teacher. She has lectured to and talked with many groups of adults and young people, and understands just what it is they want to learn about art. Miss Moore lives in Cleveland, Ohio, and spends summers on Deer Isle, on the coast of Maine. This is her first book.

1   2   3   4   5   72   71   70   69   68